Early Bird
The Power of Investing Young

Dedicated to my mother and father.

In memory of Sam Davidson. He made a large impact on many people's lives.
Rest in peace.

Even the best investors lose money sometimes. If it is money you need to pay for college or school or housing, do not invest it in stocks. Only invest money in stocks that you do not need for the next three to five years, at least. Stocks can go up, but they can also go down. That is what scares off most people.

When you think about the risk of losing money, investing can start to sound like gambling. With gambling, you have no control over winning or losing; it is random chance.

Solid investing is in no way gambling. If you do your research and buy quality companies at fair prices, then you aren't throwing your money away to a random chance. *Early Bird* will help guide you. Always do your research, understand the companies you are buying, and be prepared to hold them a long time.

Disclosure: I am not a financial advisor. Although I talk about specific companies, I do so solely for educational purposes. Always do your own research and form your own thoughts about the company.

TABLE OF CONTENTS

Why the Early Bird is Afraid of the Worm 9

Why I Invest 14
   Investor Stories 23
      Interview with David Kretzmann 23
      Interview with LouAnn Lofton 32

Company Ethics...38
   Investor Stories 43
      Interview with Alyce Lomax..................43

Economic Snowball Fight....................................51
   Investor Stories 58
      Interview with Todd Wenning 58
      Interview with Bill Mann.......................63

Metrics 68

The Power of Compounding 98

The People of the Investing World 103
   David Gardner 103
   Aunt Ginny 107

Accounts 115
   Types of Accounts..115
   One Click Away...119

Getting Started 122

Your Journey 125

My Journey 126

Appendix - Case Studies 130
   Case Study 1 - Mattel and Hasbro 130
   Case Study 2 - Moats 132

Further Readings..133

Why the Early Bird is Afraid of the Worm

"It takes twenty years to build a reputation and five minutes to ruin it. If you think about that, you'll do things differently." –Warren Buffett

I interviewed a group of teens, ages 13 to 15, asking five different questions about investing. There was a range of answers, as some had very little knowledge and others were already investors.

I was most curious to discover why people don't start investing their money early. I discovered that most of the reasons boiled down to a simple answer: misconceptions.

Teenagers tended not to want to answer the questions I asked. They were almost "closed off," but what really surprised me is how they acted when the terms "investing" and "money" were brought into play. Money is a valued and a very personal subject and generally everyone quiets when it is brought up. What surprised me is that teens shut down more than adults. Many of the teenagers would apologize for their lack of knowledge on the subject and suggested that they weren't the right pick for the survey. People, especially teens, don't like to be thought of as dumb, especially when it comes to money. When there was a question they didn't know a lot about they would quickly respond, "I know how it works," without providing further details.

I want to share the anonymous answers to each question.

What are the first words that you think of when you hear the word "investing"?

Here I made a <u>wordle</u>[1] of the most common words used. I noticed that the majority of the words they chose were investing and numbers terms like market, money, ownership, etc.

Why do you or don't you invest?

As I expected, the majority of teens said they don't invest. Most would just stick to a simple answer "No, I don't have any interest in it." Luckily, some people went into more depth and I could back up my hypothesis for why teenagers don't invest. They would say, "I don't invest because I do not have the money," or "I don't understand how to invest and I have never really thought

---

[1] www.wordle.net/

about investing." Almost everyone was open to investing, starting and learning how to do so.

More than anything, this question made me realize that everyone needs to be educated on the basic misconception that investing requires a lot of money. You can start small.

The beauty of investing is watching money grow itself. I started with $100. That's it! Everyone spends money without thinking, some people on coffee, others on fidget spinners and some on Snapple. If you were to reduce your spending on those purchases you could easily save up the money you need to start investing.

What scares you about investing?

The majority of the answers had something to do with "losing money."

Everyone was scared of losing money, whether they already invest, don't have an interest in it or want to start. Losing money is a real thing, but you have to think about it in other ways than just "losing money." To learn how to play baseball or hockey or learn anything, you have to make mistakes and learn from them, and in all of those cases people have to pay for those lessons. What if people thought of losing money in an investment (especially early on with small amounts of money) as a lesson? They would learn what went wrong, what to look for, what to avoid. Having a potential risk of losing money when you invest is a lesson to learn, not a price to pay.

What do you know about investing?

Only two people said, "not much" or "not a lot." The common answer was somewhere along the lines of, "I know it involves putting money into a company or a product and getting some of its revenue but that's about it." Those are the basics, so yes! By the end of this book, you will know enough to start investing. The next step would be expanding your knowledge of investing to help you develop your investing style. All you need to start is a computer to research companies, a small amount of money that can come from anywhere (selling dolls, a job, etc.), and a broker.

Why is it important to invest?

Many said, "because it's the most effective way to gain money," (who said teenagers aren't smart?!) but there were some who didn't know. Another answer was "you get a sense of what is happening in the world and you can make money without having to do physical labor." Each answer that was given showed me that everyone was on the right track; they knew the basics. They just needed a little more information.

Teenagers don't like being doubted or talked down to. We don't like talking about things we don't know. This book will try to clear up misconceptions. Misconceptions of the investing world are the reason that people feel a barrier of complexity, preventing us (or anyone) from entering.

As I mentioned before, a big misconception that I run into all the time is that "investing takes a lot of money."

Or "you have to be rich to invest." Investing doesn't take a lot of money, I started with only $100. Five years ago, I sold my American Girl dolls. I took half of the proceeds and invested in Mattel (MAT) and invested the other half in Hasbro (HAS). My parents and I have a deal that whatever I put in they'll match. Here we are five years later, and I have earned a total of $288.

Teenagers, more than anyone, should be educated in this field. Why? Because they have the power of time!

Warren Buffett has a famous saying, "Life is like a snowball. The important thing is wet snow and a really long hill." Although he refers to *life* as a snowball, it also applies to investing. The hill in his quote, refers to time (the more time, the better) and wet snow is strong companies. As a snowball rolls down a hill it collects more snow (as long as the snow is wet), making the snowball increase in size. So, the earlier the snowball starts, the better, because the longer it is rolling the larger it gets.

Why I Invest

"Invest in yourself. Your career is the engine of your wealth." -Paul Clitheroe

"I thought you had to go to New York and yell at people to get money. I was so mad because it cost so much to fly out there," says Isak Dai, teenage investor and quiz bowl enthusiast. Even as a 10-year-old the only barrier he felt preventing him from entering the stock market was paying for a plane ticket to get to Wall Street. If losing money crossed his mind, which it rarely did, he quickly shook it off "I am still a child so it's not like my life is on the line." That is another plus of starting young; you have less to lose. Because you are not investing your life savings into a variety of companies, there is not as big of a threat or chance for one to panic and sell. The gift of time allows you to bounce back and learn from mistakes.

Isak took a leap of faith in the stock market of Southeast Asia and Africa. He was intrigued by the world's emerging markets because of "their potential to grow explosively and provide massive return on investment *if* you're patient." His interest triggered him to buy mutual funds all around the world, but he had to learn the importance of patience.

Four years after becoming a shareholder, he sold his shares of his African Mutual Fund and is watching his Southeast Asian Mutual Fund rebound from a heartbreaking drop. But Isak is far from discouraged from his losses; he continues to track emerging markets and learn from his mistakes.

"Investing in the stock market is the best way to make money because it is the most efficient way to make money outside of working and it gives you money that you can rely on. The stock market is the best way for your money to be growing, rather than sitting there in a savings account or slowly growing in a bond." Before you start investing you need a motivation, and Isak had that, with his excitement to jump on to the next emerging market.

There is one question every investor should answer for themselves, "Why do I invest?" The first thing that popped into my mind was to make money, financial freedom. Merriam Webster defines investing, "to commit (money) in order to earn a financial return."

Is investing just about making money? I believe it is more than that. Making money is an essential part of investing. To me, the second definition of investing "to involve or engage especially emotionally" is just as important. A large part of investing is the emotional attachment. Investors follow companies, help them grow by buying shares, and should pick them based on their values. That is a very large part of why I invest. That idea can be boiled down to four reasons.

The Investing Way

The main reason I invest is because of the lifestyle and my hopes for my future. I'm not talking about fancy caviar or a nice house in the Caribbean. The stereotypical investor is usually summed up by things like that, but my experience has shown me that the opposite is true. All of the amazing investors I have met over the years share three traits: humility, frugality and nerdiness. Investing changes your mindset and impression of money. You learn to become analytical and develop good sense of humor. Mistakes will be made, so it's good to have a sense of humor and to learn from them.

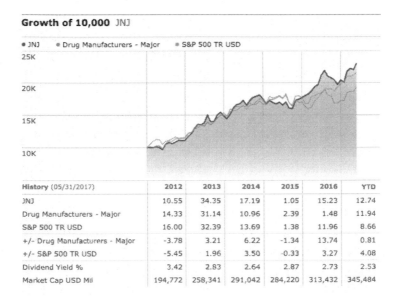

Growth of 10,000 JNJ

● JNJ   ● Drug Manufacturers - Major   ● S&P 500 TR USD

History (05/31/2017)	2012	2013	2014	2015	2016	YTD
JNJ	10.55	34.35	17.19	1.05	15.23	12.74
Drug Manufacturers - Major	14.33	31.14	10.96	2.39	1.48	11.94
S&P 500 TR USD	16.00	32.39	13.69	1.38	11.96	8.66
+/- Drug Manufacturers - Major	-3.78	3.21	6.22	-1.34	13.74	0.81
+/- S&P 500 TR USD	-5.45	1.96	3.50	-0.33	3.27	4.08
Dividend Yield %	3.42	2.83	2.64	2.87	2.73	2.53
Market Cap USD Mil	194,772	258,341	291,042	284,220	313,432	345,484

I encourage you to seek out an investor and walk around in a mall or marketplace with them. Most professional investors are happy to answer any questions a student has. One of my favorite questions is "What is your favorite stock and why?" As an investor, the world becomes a candy shop filled with tempting companies and stores to choose from. What do you notice about the store? Are there lines out the door, overflowing parking lots, or do you notice empty parking lots and employees with too much time on their hands?

You get to think about what might be a potential investment. You start to notice about the names of the sides of the train cars, or the soap dispensers or who owns your favorite ice cream brand.

While walking into town with my father we had to decide on a restaurant we wanted to go to. We narrowed it down to two options: Chipotle or a local restaurant. Before we made our choice, we considered which one had the competitive advantage. We concluded that they couldn't be compared to each other in that way. One is a local company, meaning residents in my area would know what it is and probably prefer it over Chipotle, but if non-locals were driving by they would most likely go to Chipotle. They both have lasted a long time across the street from each other and neither show any sign of leaving.

Investing opens your eyes to what makes a good business and investment. Looking at this everyday example, we were evaluating which one of the restaurants would be a better business. The world gives you clues and an investor is like a detective who has an endless series of mysteries to try and solve.

Making Your Money Work for You

Once you have put the time and effort into finding a good company, you can sit back and watch it grow. How simple is that?

Here's an example: Four years ago, I bought Johnson & Johnson (JNJ). I bought Johnson & Johnson because I'm a dancer and I would use their toe tape on a daily basis.

My original investment was $300 that grew to $460. I earned the $300 from babysitting, but I decided to make it grow. So, investing has increased my earnings by 65% and I have made a total of $160.

I chose to invest for one reason: My shares of Johnson & Johnson will likely continue to grow until I sell, while I have to work more shifts if I want to make more babysitting money. My profits from babysitting were $300 but if I invest that money, depending on how long I hold the stock, my money could double or triple or more! And if you can do both, invest and work. Win-win!

Starting off	$300
Year 1	$330
Year 2	$363
Year 3	$399.30
Year 4	$439.23
Year 5	**$458.16**
Year 6	$503.98
Year 7	$554.38
Year 8	$609.82
Year 9	$667.80
Year 10	$734.58
Year 11	$808.04
Year 12	$888.84
Year 13	$977.72
Year 14	$1,075.50
Year 15	$1,183.05
Year 16	$1,301.36
Year 17	$1,431.50
Year 18	$1,574.64
Year 19	$1,732.10
Year 20	$1,905.32

Now let's see from the original $300, how much it could grow over the next 20 years if it remains growing at the same rate. The bolded year is the current year we're on.

From this table, you can see that after 20 years of compounding I would have almost $2,000. If you subtract the original $300 that I invested, that makes $1,605.32 in investing profit.

Put simply, once you do a little work for your money, you can make your money work for you.

How Much You Learn

With investing, you can also learn more than just how to make a customer happy (although that is a big part of business); you can learn how businesses run, learn which ones succeed and find the ones that don't. Learning more about how businesses run can help you in the investing world, but it also helps with tricks of the trade if you want to start your own business.

When you invest, you learn how to make your money work for you. And you can learn patience which is the key to investing. Looking back at Johnson & Johnson I made $160 over four years, which boils down to $40 each year, but that money can go from that original investment of $300 and grow up to numbers much higher.

Like I said, I started off investing in Johnson & Johnson because I'm a dancer. They sell medical tape that many dancers use. I went through about one roll a week, meaning over 52 weeks at a cost of $3.99, they made $207.48 from one customer and one product by the end of the year. That sounded amazing to me, so I decided to invest. Now I know that investing in Johnson & Johnson is a great investment for many more reasons than just their toe tape margins.

For one thing, they are one of two American companies with AAA credit ratings (the other company is Microsoft). AAA credit rating is the accountability of the company with paying back debt and managing their money. Only 15 states have a AAA credit rating. Even our own U.S. government has a AA+ credit rating. This shows how safe and responsible Johnson & Johnson is with their money. Because investing deals with money, and we all know how precious money is, it is best to find companies with good credit ratings. They provide a blanket of comfort around your holdings and money. You can easily find a company's credit rating by looking it up on Google.

Connecting Stories and Numbers

Investing ties two of my two favorite things together; stories and number. Successful investors successfully connect the dots between the stories and numbers of a company. For me, this is the part that is the most fun. If you look at a company's numbers and see their debt is increasing, as the investor it's up to you to know why that is. Maybe it's because they have a new building being built, or they're changing headquarters, or maybe it's because they are buying another company.

Connecting the dots between the numbers and the story is what makes investors comfortable and confident in their holdings, so when they see that debt go up or the Price to Earnings Ratio go up, they do the research to know the reasons. It makes for less risky, more understandable investments.

Investing has changed me as a person and consumer. It's not for everyone, but I'm proud being the nerd I am. There are so many reasons to start and continue investing. And as Aunt Ginny (who you'll meet in a later chapter) says, "It's much better than slaving in a hamburger place."

What is your story? Why do you invest?

Investor Stories

Interview with David Kretzmann

<u>David Kretzmann</u>[2] is a living, breathing example of a young investor who started small and now has a successful career as a full-time compounder. David was born and raised in a meditation and yoga community in California. David started investing in stocks at the age of 12 years old. David graduated from Berea College with a degree in marketing and is a graduate of The Motley Fool's Analyst Development Program. Today, he serves as an investment analyst and portfolio manager for the Fool's *Rule Breakers* and *Supernova* services. He lives in Alexandria, Virginia, and is an avid runner, traveler, and loves playing and watching basketball.

How did you start investing?

"When I was 12 years old, I started looking over my dad's shoulder as he read copies of *Stock Advisor* and *Hidden Gems* -- stock recommendation newsletters from The Motley Fool. I kept asking him questions about what a stock is, how you can own a piece of a company, and what it means to invest. I was especially fascinated by the idea that I could own a piece of a business.

I had saved up $700 doing different odd jobs, like mowing lawns and playing the hammered dulcimer at Christmas fairs, and was naturally a saver rather than a spender. Now that I was getting interested in stocks, my dad set up a custodial account for me so I could invest

---

[2] www.fool.com/author/7893/index.aspx

my own money. He gave me complete autonomy of the account; from the beginning, I was investing my own money, deciding which companies to buy, and was the one to "pull the trigger" to buy or sell a stock."

What was the first company you invested in? Do you remember the reasoning behind that purchase?

"I invested my $700 in a basket of roughly 10 stocks to start out, since my brokerage at the time (Sharebuilder) allowed users to buy partial shares of companies. I started by finding the recommendations in The Motley Fool's newsletters that resonated with me and caught my interest. A couple of initial companies I remember investing in are 7-Eleven and Netflix, mainly because I was familiar with those names and brands. Thankfully I still own some of those Netflix shares today!"

Why did you decide to continue to invest? What hooked you?

"It was all so much fun. I loved the process of trying to uncover the businesses that will be future winners, and being able to actually buy shares and *own* a piece of those businesses was just the cherry on top. I found it incredibly fun -- and still do -- to learn about businesses and the world."

Did your investing style change from when you started to now? What influenced it?

"When I started out, my savings were limited and I was somewhat limited in my ability to add new money to my investment account. The majority of money that I earned from my various jobs in junior high and high school went straight toward buying stocks. When I got excited about a new stock -- which happened a lot -- I would either have to wait to buy it once I earned more cash to add to my account or sell a current holding to raise enough cash.

Now that I have a regular paycheck and can add to my investment account on a regular basis, I don't have the same pressure to pick and choose which current holdings to keep or sell. I can comfortably hold my current stocks and still have the cash to buy a new stock that I like.

My general investing style has stayed the same for the most part, in terms of thinking like a business owner and investing in companies that I want to hold for many years and decades.

In many ways, my investing style as a 12 or 13-year-old was even better than what my investing style evolved into in my early adult years. When I was younger, I focused on simple businesses that I could understand and grasp and if there was a business I didn't fully understand at first, I would do a lot of digging to understand the key drivers that would make the business successful (or not). I generally stuck with companies that were profitable and had what I felt was a reasonable chance to double in value over the next five years (which equates to about a 15% annualized return).

As an adult, I became less disciplined with the stocks I bought. I started to invest in more complex companies that were harder to understand and follow over time. This makes it harder to know what to do when a company hits hard times. Do you buy more? Do you hold? Do you sell? When it's a company you don't really understand to begin with, it will be impossible to intelligently answer those questions.

I'm trying to get back to thinking like I did as a 13-year-old, because I believe sticking with companies you can understand -- and are committed to following -- is a far better way to invest. Adults can get overconfident and make questionable investing decisions, in a way that most 13 year olds are too smart and humble to get into in the first place. In my experience, adults make things more complicated than they need to be -- and their returns suffer as a result."

The best part about starting young is the companies you know are simple ones. As you get older, when you try to go back and think like that, it is much harder. Not only that, but when you grow older and become a more experienced investor some think it is best to invest in more complicated companies. But simpler is better: That is called the <u>Humility Curve</u>.

If you went back and had to tell yourself one thing as advice as a learning investor what would it be?

"Be patient and hold your stocks -- especially your winners. In other words, commit to holding companies that you buy. Only invest in companies that you believe in and want to follow for the next five years and beyond. You won't get multi-bagger returns by jumping in and out of stocks and jumping ship at the first sight of trouble. My costliest mistake as an investor has been selling future winners too early (Buffalo Wild Wings, Monster Beverage, Chipotle, Netflix, and many more)."

Do you think investing shaped you as a person? In what way(s)?

"Investing has helped me look at the world as an owner and a stakeholder, rather than going through life as a passive consumer. Investing has also reinforced the importance of being patient and calm even when a lot of other people are panicking or worrying about the latest headlines. It's helped me stay levelheaded and focused on the long term -- not just with stocks, but life in general."

It is true investing nudges you to learn about a lot of things, money, math, but most importantly, the world. What happens in the world affects the stock's performance -- a new consumer trend, a President's decision that might hinder a company's profit.

How did you learn to use the Motley Fool to learn and grow as an investor?

"As soon as I started investing, each day I would log on to the Fool's website and spend hours reading articles and browsing the discussion boards. After a few months of this, I asked my dad if I could use his account to begin posting on the discussion boards. Being the sport that he was, he quickly replied, "Sure, I'm not using it!"

I hopped onto the discussion boards and started analyzing companies and answering questions people had about stocks and investing. People seemed to like what I was posting, so the volume and length of my posts kept going up. I didn't think it was important to disclose I was 13 (minor details).

Someone from the Fool reached out to me to see if I would be interested in becoming a contractor, at which point I finally had to disclose my age. To the credit of the Fool and its community, people were supportive and encouraging when they found out I was just a youngster who loved stocks and investing. The Fool even wrote an article about me that was posted on the homepage of AOL for a time (when AOL was still semi-relevant). When I was 14, my dad and I flew to Fool HQ in Alexandria, Virginia, and met with Fool cofounders David and Tom Gardner and a team of analysts. Stocks and investing were the centerpieces of my world as a teen."

What do you think is the fear with investing? What prevents people from getting started investing at younger ages?

"To quote Fool cofounder David Gardner, "People make fearful that which they don't understand." A lot of factors can go into why some people are afraid or skeptical about investing in stocks. Some people grew up through periods where they might have seen the stock market crash and subsequently decided to stick with very conservative investment alternatives like bonds or CDs for the rest of their lives. Other people try schemes like buying "pump-and-dump" penny stocks and soon can't tell the difference between the stock market and a casino.

Since most kids still don't learn much about investing in school, they are out of luck if their parents or other family members don't introduce them to the world of stocks. In my case, it was thanks to my dad that I was introduced to investing and encouraged each step of the way. Without his influence and guidance, there is no way I would have started investing as early as I did. Most kids are in a similar boat, where they just need a family member or teacher to help get them started on the path to investing -- but that's still not very common, unfortunately."

How do you think parents, schools, and clubs can help support kids to get started?

"I think an effective "hook" to pique the interest of kids is introducing the concept of being able to own a piece of the companies behind their favorite brands or products. The idea that they can be not only a consumer, but also an *owner* and participate in the success of companies and brands that they know and love like Netflix, Starbucks, Apple, Disney, and many others can be motivating to kids.

It's still a code that needs to be cracked. Schools and clubs can help kids follow businesses over the course of a semester or year. It should be kept simple and approachable, which is why I prefer helping kids make the connection between brands/products and businesses. Once you have that concept down the stock market becomes less intimidating and a lot more fun."

What do you believe is the target age to get kids/teens investing?

"The basic mechanics and value of money can be introduced at an early age, and kids can start investing at least by the time they're in middle school. A parent or teacher might need to be more hands-on depending on the kid, but there is no need to for investing to be any more complicated than what a middle schooler can grasp. The earlier they get started the better!"

Teens, but anyone actually, can get bored with this topic. Do you believe it will always be like this or will more people learn to be passionate about investing?

"Not everyone will necessarily treat investing like a hobby, but there is a lot we can do to help teens -- and people of all ages -- get more comfortable with the stock market and how to invest. Even if someone doesn't find investing in stocks to be as fun or exciting as we do, they should still save and invest. I don't mind if someone doesn't want to devote a lot of time to investing, so long as they still invest. At the very least, people should be excited about investing as a means toward ends like becoming financially independent, having money to give to causes they believe in, and building a secure financial future."

David brings up another great point about saving versus spending. You have to save before you spend, which is difficult for some but for others it comes naturally. Learning the power of saving money is very important and one of the best ways to do it is through investing!

The best way to get kids to invest (and almost anything) is to show them the potential of that hobby, career, and effort. David is a very good example of what can happen if you start out young. You have the time to learn from your mistakes, compound, and build a career (if you want).

Interview with LouAnn Lofton

LouAnn Lofton has been proudly investing "like a girl" since she was young. She was an early, self-taught learner with an inspirational story.
She learned about the power of compounding and became a confident investor which brought her to The Motley Fool in 2000, where she rose to the position of managing editor of Fool.com—an award-winning financial education website visited by more than five million people each month. *Warren Buffett Invests Like A Girl* is her first book and the one that allowed her to finally meet her investment idol, Warren Buffett

How did you start investing? What interested you?

"I didn't grow up investing or even learn about it as a kid. It wasn't something we talked about in my family. However, when I turned 21, I inherited some money from a life insurance policy that my father had. Unfortunately, he'd died suddenly when I was just 14. The money I received from that policy wasn't a ton, but it was enough that I worried about what to do with it, and frankly, didn't trust myself not to just spend it all. After doing some research, investing in the market seemed to be the way to go.

But that still left a huge gap in my actual knowledge of how to go about investing, so I read just about everything I could find. I explored day trading, momentum investing, the CANSLIM strategy from

Investor's Business Daily, even commodities and futures. It all struck me as incredibly complicated.

Then, I came across a biography of this guy Warren Buffett. This was the early-mid 1990s, and while Buffett was well known in some financial circles, he wasn't quite the ubiquitous figure he is today. I'd never heard of him before reading that book and what I discovered opened my eyes to a way of investing that I believed I could both understand and succeed at.

Here was a guy who ignored the day-to-day movements of the market, who situated himself in his hometown of Omaha, far away from Wall Street's hubbub, and who professed that he invested in what he could understand, with a goal of holding onto it forever. He thought long-term, as opposed to the very short-term thinking I'd encountered in most other things I'd read.

Around that same time, I also read Peter Lynch's books, describing his own investing strategy, which meshed in some ways with Buffett's. Notably, from both Lynch and Buffett, I took to heart the idea of beginning my investing by focusing on companies that I knew well and could understand the financial prospects of.

I still think that is a valuable way for investors, especially novice ones, to approach things. Without a doubt, you have to dig into a company's financials and do your due diligence overall, but starting that process with companies you know and love makes sense to me. I discovered some of my earliest investments, companies I still hold, this way."

What misconceptions surround investing and how does that prevent people (of all ages) from starting?

"I think the primary misconception that trips people up is that investing is just too complex for them to understand, unless they are some whiz kid with an advanced degree working on Wall Street. There are lots of incentives for investment professionals to make people feel this way, so no wonder it works.

It's a shame, because as we know, the earlier you get started investing, the better. Time is your most important asset here.

I think people also often don't realize how much of investing is not about picking the perfect stock at the perfect time, but is instead, about managing your own emotions. Having the optimal portfolio won't help if you get shaken out of your positions whenever the market hiccups. This is another lesson I took to heart from Buffett. Temperament matters, in a big way. Staying patient, controlling risk, and keeping the long-term view in mind go so far, much farther than lots of folks realize, in making you a successful investor. (In fact, temperament matters so much I wrote a whole book about it!)"

That's a good point. The timing is important, but learning to manage your emotions is a crucial skill. Many know the saying, "Buy low, sell high." But how many actually do that? It is much easier to verbalize that action than it is to stop yourself from a panic attack during the '08 market crash.

Personally, <u>Socially Responsible Investing (SRI)</u> is hooking me right now, but do you have a certain sector of the market or focus that interests you?

"I'd say SRI for me, too. SRI is fascinating and I think will be a big thing for a long, long time, especially as more young people get involved in investing. I also like that you can look at it through a lens of different industries and sectors, so if you don't feel confident about your circle of competence in, say, energy, you can find SRI companies in other areas that you do know more about."

What was the first company you invested in?

"Nike. And I still own those shares more than 20 years later. Starbucks was another early one for me, and I still own those shares, too."

Over 20 years Starbucks (SBUX) has grown around 2,152% and Nike (NKE) has grown around 624%.

How has your investing style changed from when you started?

"It honestly hasn't changed all that much. I developed, over the years, an ability to be a patient, long-term investor. That's not to say, at all, that that mindset is easy to maintain. But I've had two significant tests of it -- the market's down in 2000 and again in the fall of 2008/2009. I didn't panic and sell either time. I'm still learning, though. Being an investor is a lifelong pursuit."

If you went back and had to tell yourself one thing as advice as a learning investor what would it be?

"Be braver about buying more shares of companies you believe in when the market offers them up at a discount. I'm good about not selling. I'm trying to get better about the flip side of that. (Or, in Buffett speak, I'm trying to learn to be greedier when others are fearful.)"

LouAnn Lofton started out young and had to learn a lot on her own to get to where she is now. I picked out a few important points that I found incredibly valid.

Throughout her thoughtful answers, she mentions emotional control. As an investor, that is a very important skill. Investors make their money from self-control. Buying at a low, and selling at a high. A better way to think about a downfall in the market is a sale at a store. Rather than paying $100 for new jeans, you are gifted the sale so you only have to pay $20. Do your own research, there could be a problematic reason that those jeans (or company) is on sale. Always do a background check. That's the same with stocks.

Another point LouAnn mentioned is how much money it took for her to start investing. It is a big misconception that you have to have a lot of money to start investing. Investing doesn't take a lot of money to start. The point is to save your money and make your money work for you. All you need is a seed to get started. Just like a job, it takes work, time, effort, and a little bit of money to apply for a job, so does investing. Investing is important for more than just making money. It helps you learn to manage your money in a way that makes you feel comfortable.

Don't Forget!
- Investing is a way to make your money work for you.
- Holding companies you understand will help you during challenging times.

Company Ethics

"Know what you own and why you own it."
- Peter Lynch

I used to think that the hardest thing about investing was the battle between my personal values and making a profit. As investors, we all want to make money and sometimes we think that our values have to become an afterthought of that. Thinking back to the dictionary definition of the verb, invest, it means "to commit (money) in order to earn a financial return." That is what most investors go for. And as I said, I believe it is so much more than just "making money". To me, investing, as Merriam Webster uses in their second definition, is "to involve or engage especially emotionally."

Investing is not solely about making money; it is about investing in your values in the future. Socially Responsible Investing (SRI) lines up your values and personal beliefs with your purchases and investments. SRI means you invest in companies that line up with your values, for example: they treat their workers fairly or are environmentally conscious.

How do you rate companies on whether they are good citizens? Environmental, Social and Governance (ESG) are three categories that a lot of people use to judge the social responsibility of a company.

The ESG categories create guidelines based on your values.

The ESG categories are helpful tools to screen companies for what you are looking for or what you are looking to avoid. You can screen companies in two ways, negative and positive. Negative screening is eliminating companies to invest in based on values that you *don't agree* with.

Here is an example of some personal values that come to mind, although you don't have to agree with them. These are some common personal choices of what people use for negative screening:

Environment	Social	Governance
Chemicals and agrochemicals Biocides Controversial environmental behavior	Pornography Alcohol Tobacco Gambling Animal testing Exploitation of child labor	Systematic lobbying of public institutions Corruption

Next is positive screening. Positive screening is the opposite of negative screening, instead of eliminating companies you disagree with. Positive screening you look for companies that promote values that you *do agree* with.

Environment	Social	Governance
Wind power Solar power Nuclear power	LGBTQ+ rights Women's rights Black Lives Matter	Giving shareholders a say Ethical managers and board members

Here are some key things to think about for SRI:

Long Term Mindset

SRI seems pretty logical: Invest based on your values. So why don't people do it? For one thing, not all investors are long term investors. For some environmental and social impacts, you need to think 30, 40, or 50 years out. Some people don't have that time, so it is much safer for them to invest in companies that will be popular next week, rather in the next 30 years.

Adapting to Generation Gaps

Over the next 20-30 years, generational wealth transfer will happen, and signs point to a large shift of mindset towards socially responsible investing. When the torch is passed to the next generations, the companies that investors invest in will have much different values.

World of Change

For investors, SRI is a great opportunity to invest while the companies don't have a high stock price. For some trends, you may need to have a lot of time, some because they are developing a new drug, others because switching to green energy sources takes time, money, etc. Now the issue with having to maintain faith in a company for a long time is you can only predict so far into the future. For most companies, two years is hard to predict; 50 is much harder (almost impossible). That is a big struggle for investors to realize that it'll be a risk now, but may be beneficial and profitable later. Some of these companies might only be an idea now, or forming in someone's basement. Our goal, as investors, is to keep our eyes open for these companies and pounce as soon as possible.

Personal Values Connection

Most investors keep their private life and investing separate. Being socially responsible is something most people think of as driving their car less, turning lights off when they leave the room, not running water when you don't need it, etc., but investing can make as equal, if not a bigger impact on the future. You have the power of your voice, your wallet, and your stock portfolio along with power over your actions.

When you become a shareholder, you are part owner of that company. You can vote on that company's decisions. Of course, there's only so much you can do with that vote, but with ownership comes power. You have the power to put your money in companies you believe in. As David Gardner says, "Invest in the world you want to see 10, 20, or 30 years from now."

Don't Forget!
- ESG (Environmental, Social, Governance) are the three categories most investors use to value a company. Most companies will not succeed in all three.
- There are two types of screening, negative and positive.
  - Positive screening is looking for companies that promote your values.
  - Negative screening is eliminating companies that are against your values.
- SRI (Socially Responsible Investing) takes time; therefore, it also takes patience, adaptability, and the ability to connect your personal values to your holdings.
- SRI is about the long term and investing is too.

Investor Stories

Interview with Alyce Lomax

In search of more information on SRI (Socially Responsible Investing), I interviewed Alyce Lomax[3]. Alyce Lomax has been in the financial news and information industry for about 25 years; she has spent nearly 15 of those years at The Motley Fool, where she is currently an analyst and writer focused on sustainable investing in all its forms.

What does SRI mean to you? What does ESG (Environmental, Social, Governance) mean to you?

SRI involves screening out certain stocks and industries on ethical grounds. To my way of thinking, ESG integration involves including environmental, social, and governance attributes in investing theses, whether it's to uncover enhanced opportunities along those lines (for example, an excellent culture adding up to a competitive advantage, or sustainable products that result in greater sales or illustrate major innovation), or to assess risks (such as lawsuits, regulatory risks, and so forth). I feel that when I'm investing, I use a hybrid approach -- there are some industries and companies I refuse to invest in on ethical grounds -- they're just automatically screened out for me -- although I am open to changing my mind if some companies might be able to move the needle on important areas like sustainability.

---

[3] www.my.fool.com/profile/TMFLomax/activity.aspx

When it comes to investing in your values do you always have to sacrifice something (making less OR forgoing your values)?

I don't believe investors have to sacrifice! These days, there are more and more companies that are doing great work in making their businesses more sustainable, stakeholder-centric, and so forth. The range of choices we can make of companies to invest in while keeping our values in mind is expanding. Of course, it also helps to be a patient, long-term investor buying shares of high-quality, well-managed companies -- and often, those kinds of companies are stakeholder-centric.

Do you have any examples of a company that shows a good balance of making money and is socially responsible?

There are plenty of choices these days! Starbucks and Costco are two of my favorite examples right off the top of my head, particularly in the employee treatment area, and long-time shareholders most certainly can't complain about how well those stocks have performed over the course of years.

Is it better to have a split portfolio that consists of SRI companies and ones that don't follow your values, or stick to one option or the other?

I think that for many investors to be able to fully sleep at night, they'd want to stick to SRI portfolios or companies. Then again, I can see how some folks might have situations where they are actively picking stocks along SRI lines but their company doesn't offer a socially responsible 401(K) options, for example. That said, more and more funds are integrating some ESG elements into their methodologies. It's also worth it for people in that situation to check into what stocks their funds are buying, and if they have issues with some of them, contact their fund providers and ask them if they engage with some of those companies on those issues, and if they are voting their shares for SRI/sustainable shareholder resolutions. For example, 62% of ExxonMobil shareholders recently voted in favor of a climate impact report shareholder resolution -- that means a lot of the big funds used their firepower to ask the company to better address the climate change issue.

Is it more effective to do negative screening (elimination of values you disagree with) or positive screening (focusing only on certain areas) when finding stocks?

As I said before, I really like doing a bit of a hybrid of the two versions. Personally, I find that having some industries I'm just not going to consider frees me to focus on other companies in other industries that may be doing amazing things but might not be too obvious. There are so many different ways people can do SRI -- and that also includes shareholder activism, where one can buy shares of a company that they think needs to change for the better of some or all stakeholders and conduct shareholder activism and submit shareholder proposals for other investors to vote upon.

Is it alright if a company isn't quite to where you would like it to be, in terms of SRI, but is heading there?

I think so, but of course, it's up to each investor to decide where they will draw the line as to where "good enough" socially responsible behavior is. I really like a lot of things Pepsi has been doing in sustainability and dedicating R&D spending to formulating new, healthier products so that it offers its customers tons of choices (including choices that are better for them!). However, plenty of SRI investors would say that Pepsi still basically offers junk food and sugar water that help create public health problems, and that's not OK and should be screened out.

Looking at the average investor, do you think more investors lean towards SRI or investing just to make money? Why do they lean to one side or another? What benefits does the individual investor derive from SRI?

There is a sea change going on -- there are more and more socially responsible investors (regardless of what they call themselves, since there are so many names for it these days!). According to US SIF, last year $8.72 trillion in assets under management in the United States were devoted to Socially Responsible Investing/Environmental, Social, Governance strategies. Millennials, and your yet-unnamed generation, are leading the way! That said, there are still many, many investors who don't believe you should mix your personal values and your investing. I think that one of the biggest reasons for that is they have bought the conventional wisdom that you can't make money that way, or that investing that way is only "political." There's a ton of data out there that shows that socially responsible investing does not guarantee one will lose money, and oftentimes investors can do just as well or better financially. Also, let's not forget the ESG integration element involves mitigating risk -- if a company that's been hurting stakeholders in the blind, irresponsible pursuit of short-term shareholder value blows up and the stock collapses, well, they've lost money. I think people don't always realize SRI/ESG is a way to try to avoid downside risk.

Can you make a change in the world by starting SRI?

I believe people can and they are making changes in the world by investing this way! Again, young folks are making it clear they want to buy sustainable and socially responsible products, work for sustainable and socially responsible companies, and invest in sustainable and socially responsible stocks. The marketplace is evolving to reflect that demand -- in just one example, according to the Governance & Accountability Institute, 82% of S&P 500 companies published a sustainability report last year, up from just under 20% in 2011.

Have you ever spoken up to a company about a decision they are making that you disagree with? What is the importance of that?

As an analyst and writer for The Motley Fool for almost 15 years, I have written plenty of articles about decisions companies' managements make that I disagree with, including some that I own and like and even consider pretty socially responsible! There is no perfect company and I do think it's important to make stands on certain issues and ask the right questions, even question our own theses. I have of course also at times voted my proxy ballots for shareholder resolutions that ask for changes in areas having to do with sustainability, CEO compensation, etc. I generally don't directly contact companies or their management teams, but I think investors should always remember they can ring up their companies' investor relations departments and voice an opinion on issues. Taking a stand on important issues makes a difference in the world.

Investing with good ethics is logical. Why do you think people don't do it?

Again, I think the conventional wisdom that it's a money-losing venture colors the decision, as well as the politicization of thinking about far-ranging impacts businesses have on the world, for the good or the bad. Talking about values and ethics shouldn't feel like something that's inappropriate for polite conversation. In addition, I think some folks construe concern for stakeholders and externalized costs as a weakness instead of a strength in the marketplace. That's sad, because ultimately, we are talking about what is positive and sustainable in the economic sense or not.

Warren Buffett has said: "You have certain things you want to achieve, but if you don't have the love and respect of people, you are always a failure. That is the one thing you must earn, it can never be bought. No one that has the love and respect of others is ever a failure." Do you believe, if we educated people on the "popularity" of good ethics, more people would invest in a socially responsible manner?

I love that quote. I think that's a great point that maybe ethical behavior should be viewed as the thing the cool kids are doing, so to speak. And how people view the companies one owns is no joke: if a whole lot of people hate a company, root for it to go down, and wouldn't miss it if it went away, not only is it not one to feel particularly proud of, but it's also a heck of a lot riskier than ones that are respected, admired, and trusted.

Living a socially responsible life is becoming more and more important and it will soon show in the companies we invest in.

Alyce mentions one company in which I have a personal investing story- Pepsi. At the time of my purchase of Pepsi shares, I was reading, *Omnivore's Dilemma* by Michael Pollan[4]. This book is about many things related to a healthy, balanced diet. The purpose of Pollan's book is to make people more aware of their diets and health choices, in that he bashed a lot of food brands that I

---

[4]www.amazon.com/Omnivores-Dilemma-Natural-History-Meals/dp/0143038583

knew: Pepsi, Coca-Cola, and Nestle. Even as a 6th grader, I realized this is where the world was heading and as an investor you want to stay on that same path, but what makes an investor happy is to find a company that adapts to the time and people's tastes. Pepsi has been expanding Quaker Oats, making more protein bars, and is in the process of cutting 20% of the calories from their sugary drinks. In 2016, Pepsi bought a probiotic health food company called Kevita; Naked Juice; and Aquafina, a water company. This shows that Pepsi is trying to make a difference and appeal to consumers. They learned that people want more natural options and fewer chemical additives. Consumers are becoming much more socially responsible, as are the companies. As the demand for healthier alternatives is increasing, Pepsi is changing to fit the customer's needs.

SRI is a very good way to put your money where your mouth is and speak up for changes you want to see made. Being socially responsible is where the world is heading and it's where we should put our money. SRI is a great way to jump on the train earlier and as Alyce says it's important "for many investors to be able to fully sleep at night."

Economic Snowball Fight

"If you don't have a competitive advantage,
don't compete." -Jack Welch

In 2014, I posted on The Motley Fool[5] about two toy companies, Mattel (MAT) and Hasbro (HAS). The post was called Invest Like a Girl, an American Girl[6]. I compared those two to see which was a better stock to buy at the time. In the end, I came to the conclusion that Mattel was. It had a higher dividend, high profits margins, and lower debt and a lower price (based on the P/E ratio -don't worry I will talk you through these numbers later). Those numbers would be an obvious buying point right there, but looking at those two competitors now, investors would come to a much different conclusion.

Since then, Mattel lost a deal with Disney for the production of their Disney princess dolls. That meant large sums of money that Mattel could have earned from Frozen dolls was earned by Hasbro instead.

Luckily for Hasbro, Frozen was a huge hit. The popularity of earlier princesses along with the newfound love for Elsa, Anna, and Olaf made Hasbro's sales skyrocket. Along with that, Hasbro had the long-held contract with Star Wars to produce their toys. With three movies coming out in four years, Hasbro couldn't have wished for more.

---

[5] www.fool.com/
[6] www.fool.com/investing/general/2014/07/19/invest-like-a-girl-an-american-girl.aspx

New York University's <u>Aswath Damodaran</u>[7] believes a good valuation is made with a story and numbers. You need both to find the right stock. What I lacked when I did my valuation was the story. I had the numbers, but I didn't predict Hasbro's successes because I didn't know a new Star Wars movie was going to come out, or about Mattel losing the Disney princess deal.

You can see from the chart below that Hasbro (the line above) is doing much better than Mattel.

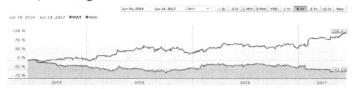

Source Morningstar

That is the past, but investing is about the future. So, what about now? Comparing the two companies now, I would say both are fair game for investors. Hasbro has jumped ahead of Mattel with yet another Star Wars movie, and with more Disney princess movies to come, they will hopefully continue on their path.

Mattel, with their new CEO (from Google), Margo Georgiadis, also has an exciting future. She is upping their technology game to make sure Mattel's products stay new and improved with digital trends. Mattel still has many well-known and popular brands (for example, Hot Wheels, Barbie, Monster High, Mega Bloks). Both Mattel and Hasbro have potential in the future that shines through on both their numbers and story.

---

[7] www.pages.stern.nyu.edu/~adamodar/

Although my prediction for those two companies was off, all investors make mistakes, and I just have to *let it go.*

You win some, you lose some. Winning more often than losing is what it is all about and investors who study competitive advantage will have an edge. Competitive advantage is a way to identify which company has the advantage over another. This concept is very important in investing because it helps separate good stocks from bad ones, winners from losers.

A company's competitive advantage is often called a moat. This is an analogy. The castle in this analogy is the business itself and the moat is the competitive advantage of the company. The moat protects the castle from outside attackers or, in this case, other competing businesses. The moat is a way for investors to identify the advantage one business has over another. In this post, I will be talking about the different types of moats and how they can be beneficial to an investor.

According to Morningstar[8], an online investment service, there are five different types of moats:
- Intangible Assets
- Customer Switching Cost
- Cost Advantage
- Network Effect
- Efficient Scale

---

[8] www.youtube.com/watch?v=XziAhR-N7D8

Before we dive in, I would like to mention the importance of a moat. Like I said, a moat is what protects one business from being overthrown by another. It is what makes consumers pick your product off the shelf instead of another. Although it is a somewhat easy concept to grasp many business owners forget. In fact, 80% of new businesses fail within the first 18 months. That could be due to their company lacking a moat.

Intangible Assets

First, one of the most common moats is Intangible Assets. This means the company has either patents protecting a service or product so it cannot be copied. For example, Coca-Cola (KO). People have been drinking Coca-Cola for around 120 years and still enjoy it. They have the brand and the name so well established that it would be nearly impossible for another company to overthrow them. And when they had an "oopsie"[9] of changing the flavor of their drink, they recovered somewhat quickly because people remembered their brand.

Customer Switching Cost

Customer Switching Cost means that leaving one company and switching to another would make a great inconvenience for the consumer or customer. Although it's called a customer switching cost, that doesn't always mean money; it can refer to time or another inconvenience. This discourages many customers from switching, unless there is a benefit of some sort, like an

---

[9] www.coca-colacompany.com/stories/coke-lore-new-coke

improvement in price or performance of the product or service. For example, growing up in the 21st century, one of the biggest decisions I've had to make is whether to buy an Android or Apple phone. It is very difficult for some people to switch services because of the different music, apps, movies, software and hardware and it doesn't transfer as smoothly. Normally, once a customer decides on their phone provider, they stick with it.

Cost Advantage

Cost Advantage is something that is very noticeable in one company in particular: Amazon (AMZN). Because of their low prices and speedy delivery people prefer to order from them causing other companies to struggle. I have watched a number of Barnes and Nobles (BKS) disappear from my city because of Amazon competition. Consumers, for the most part, look for the cheaper option of a product or service making it harder and harder for other companies to match it. For example, when you're at the grocery store and picking out ice cream, there are many options so the decision becomes a matter of which is cheaper. Consumer almost always go for the cheaper option.

Now, this doesn't always apply. Quickly looking back at Intangible Assets, shows that once you have a few, well-known brands established people are willing to pay a bit more for a known brand. An easy example of times when Intangible Assets beat Cost Advantage is Tiffany & Co (TIF). Customers are willing to pay 30% more for a Tiffany diamond rather than another branded diamond that is cheaper.

Network Effect

The Network Effect is when the product's value increases with the addition of each incremental user. This definition, I know, is a little confusing but the example might clear it up. More people get Mastercard or Visa so more merchants have to accept them. When more stores accept them, more people become cardholders. It's just one large circle of supply and demand. Another example is social media, like Facebook. The more people post, the more people join. Putting it simply, stronger companies get stronger.

Efficient Scale

Normally, when the supply and demand cycle happens it washes away smaller companies, leaving a few larger, more powerful companies. This is the last moat called Efficient Scale. That means that there is a market that is controlled by one or a few major companies. It limits other companies trying to enter the field and makes great competitive prices for the few existing companies. For example, if BNSF Railway (BRK.B) wanted to build a railroad from Minnesota to North Dakota to carry coal it would not benefit another company to come and build a parallel railway to ship the same product.

This moat doesn't apply to all types of markets, for example, the food market. When considering Chipotle (CMG) or McDonald's (MCD), I may change my opinion of which restaurant I want to go to everyday giving both companies my business. With a railroad company, you have to pick which one you want to provide the state with coal.

Once you start to use it, this list of moats should become a second language to you. It is very important to think about a company's advantages when you're trying to identify good stocks. The larger the moat, the less risky the stock is. Not only is it very beneficial to investors, but it's fun to just think about. For example, if there are two stores across the street which one will last longer because of their competitive advantage?

On Morningstar's website, they have an easily accessible moat rating, which will help you get a good idea.

Don't Forget!
- Competitive advantage is finding which company has the stronger, larger moat.
- There are five types of moats:
    - Intangible Assets: Patents surrounding the company's brand or products and brand recognition.
    - Customer Switching Cost: A fee or an inconvenience incurred is when a customer decides to switch companies.
    - Cost Advantage: Having cheaper options for customers.
    - Network Effect: When there is more demand for the product and so the value increases making it more accessible to others.
    - Efficient Scale: When the supply and demand cycle happens, it washes away smaller companies, leaving a few larger, more powerful companies.

Investor Stories

Interview with Todd Wenning

I interviewed Todd Wenning on the competitive advantage. Todd Wenning, CFA is an equity analyst at Johnson Investment Counsel. Before joining Johnson in 2015, Todd was an equity analyst at Morningstar and ran a dividend-focused newsletter for The Motley Fool UK. He is the author of *Keeping Your Dividend Edge* (2016) and his articles have been published by Morningstar, Investors Chronicle, CFA Institute, and The Motley Fool. He also has a blog, Clear Eyes Investing[10]. Todd's opinions here are his own and not necessarily those of his employer.

What does competitive advantage mean to you? How do you describe a moat (in general)?

There are two types of competitive advantages - temporary and durable. A company that sells a "fad" product, for example, might generate high profit margins and returns for a time, but eventually, competition enters, and the trend ends. Fidget spinners are a case in point. Instead, what I'm looking for as an investor are durable advantages, or "economic moats." Whereas new competitors quickly eliminate a temporary advantage, a durable advantage is something that keeps competitors from eating away at your profits for an extended period. Ideally, a moat will enable a company to generate high returns on invested capital for more than ten years. There

---

[10] www.cleareyesinvesting.com/

are four main moat sources, in my opinion - intangible assets (patents, brands, regulatory protection, etc.), switching costs, network effects, and low-cost production.

Looking at Morningstar's five main types of moats, which is most crucial for a company to have?

The importance will vary by company. For example, a commodity producer doesn't need to have a brand advantage or network effects on its side. What it wants to have, however, are low-cost production advantages. Companies with particularly wide moats typically have more than one moat source. Apple's moat, for instance, is anchored by a valuable brand (you're willing to pay up for an Apple product) and switching costs (once you're in the Apple ecosystem, it's costly in time and money to change to Android or another ecosystem). It's hard enough for a company to dig one moat, let alone two or more, so these are exceptional companies that fit this mold.

What is a good example of a moat that consumers directly experience?

As consumers, we most frequently experience intangible asset brand advantages, though this is changing in some ways due to technology. As we spend more of our lives consuming digital content, for example, we'll likely encounter more software-related moat sources like switching costs and network effects. One mistake investors make is equating a brand's market share or awareness alone as a moat source. To be a moat source, a branded product must command a higher price relative to comparable products. It also can't be explained by higher production costs alone. Even though you're well aware of GM and Ford automobiles, for instance, you're not likely willing to spend more money for the privilege of driving either one. On the other hand, luxury car manufacturers like Ferrari, BMW, and Mercedes can mark up their products because they don't just sell cars; they also sell experiences.

Why is it important for investors to know about competitive advantage? Does it give investors any advantage to know about competitive advantage?

The market often assumes - and usually correctly - that companies will experience a reversion to the mean on their returns on invested capital due to competition. No company's moat lasts forever, of course, but moats enable firms to generate higher returns on invested capital for much longer than the market likely suspects. If your assumptions about a firm's return on invested capital persisting for longer than what the market's priced in turn out to be correct, you will end up making money.

What's your favorite moat and why?

My favorite moat source is intangible assets, specifically brand. I find the psychological effects of brands to be fascinating. When I take a sip of Coke, for example, I always remember drinking Coke out of glass bottles at my late grandmother's house. There's a deep link between taste, smell, brands and memories. Buffett has noted that this is one reason why Coca-Cola wants to be everywhere fun times are happening - sporting events, concerts, amusement parks, and so on. They want to make that connection between the brand and your memories.

Thinking about moats in different types of companies - in growing companies, who want to continue to increase their margins and customer base; and for defensive companies, who may want more stability and safety, what kinds of moats are most successful in companies looking to grow versus those trying to defend their competitive position?

Interesting question. I think it varies by the type of business. If you're a growing software company, for instance, you want to establish switching costs or network effects as quickly as possible. This is why software companies tend to offer free trials to products. They want to make the software part of your daily routine so that it will be harder to stop using it when the trial ends. If you're an established consumer products company with a brand advantage, you should focus on defending that brand at all costs by investing in marketing, advertising, and innovation around it.

The power of more than one moat source leads to a longer lasting competitive advantage for the company, meaning that, while finding such companies is extremely rare, once you do you can rely on them for the long haul.

In Todd's example of Ferrari and BMW, they are selling more than just the physical product and are successful in creating an experience for their customers, which leads to a great brand – brand loyalty - and a brand can be a very powerful (perhaps the most powerful) moat. As Todd said Coca-Cola is a great example, but you can find these brands everywhere. One that sticks out to me is Mattel. Whenever that brands comes up I always think about happy little girls playing with Barbies.

Lastly, I underestimated the switching cost moat. It can be used to retain customers and is especially helpful to up-and-coming businesses. Along with technology companies like Apple, Android, etc., these switching costs apply to other companies like Verizon, AT&T, T-Mobile, etc.

Interview with Bill Mann

Bill Mann is the Director of Small Cap Research at the Motley Fool. Prior to that, he was the founding Chief Investment Officer for Motley Fool's investing arm, Motley Fool Asset Management, where he oversaw three mutual funds and seven separately managed account strategies with nearly $2 billion in assets under management. Mr. Mann has an insightful take on the fun (and power) of investing internationally. I have very minimal experience with international investments, so I'm very excited to learn more!

How do you look for competitive advantage in companies outside of the US versus internal, US-focused companies?

So, believe it or not the process is very much the same, except that in many countries there are additional types of competitive advantages that aren't available in the US. In the U.S. there are very strong rules that prevent commingling of public and private interests, but in many countries, there are companies that are provided additional protection from competitors. For example, in China online companies have been allowed to develop, like Baidu or JD.com, because the government kept out large foreign competitors. In France companies from yogurt maker, Danone to Evian, are considered strategic assets for the country.

I love companies that operate on island or island-like markets. You can find some pretty good businesses and they are, by virtue of their geography, protected from certain competitive forces. One really great example is the Bank of Greenland.

The pros of investing in small island businesses are the competition. Bill Mann talked about the Bank of Greenland. That bank is the only local commercial bank in Greenland. Meaning, other banks are less likely to try and become a competitor because the Bank of Greenland is so well established (I'd hope so since it's been around since 1967). Having one company that the whole island relies on can be extremely helpful to an investor to seeking out the right investment.

Do your investing "guidelines" differ depending on the country you're looking at?

Yes. You have to be aware that for all of its faults the US regulatory system is by and large the best in the world for protecting individual minority investors. In lots of countries (and not just emerging markets) there is literally a disincentive for the companies to uphold foreign minority shareholder rights as their court systems are quite corrupt. For example, this last year the Chinese Securities Regulatory Commission announced that it was delisting Dandong Xintai Electric for fraud, the first time they've delisted a company for fraud in nearly 7 years.

Given that more than 50 Chinese companies were delisted in the US based on alleged fraud or violation of securities laws, does it even remotely make sense that ones listed in China were paragons of virtue? Not to me.

All that said, I tend to analyze companies on the basis of their audited financial statements and then work backward from there. What I tend to do is place a country-specific additional discount rate on companies in countries I don't have as much confidence in – let's call that an *omega* discount. But at the end of the day, there are 50,000-plus publicly traded companies worldwide, so there isn't any need in reaching for any one company if you're the slightest bit suspicious.

What benefits do investors have with investing outside of the US?

The pat answer is diversification, but I don't spend much time thinking about that. The real benefit to me is that you gain access to situations that are no longer possible in the US. So, for example, Indonesia's middle class has grown fourfold in the last few decades, leading to a huge increase and shift in consumption habits. The US is a wonderful economy and I'd never bet against it, but it does not have any potential to bring so many people out of poverty in such short order. Other countries have a natural advantage in certain products and really great companies that are benefitting. For example, Malaysia is blessed with rubber, petroleum, a moderately priced workforce and a good infrastructure, which are the basic ingredients to give it an absolute advantage in the manufacture of disposable gloves.

Looking at the top five economies in the world (United States, China, Japan, Germany, United Kingdom) which types of moats do better in which economic environments? Is there a pattern?

I don't spend much time thinking about economic environments, preferring to focus on the companies themselves. That said, it is a simple fact that China and probably India will have larger economies than the US in our lifetimes, so there is a certain benefit to thinking about companies that serve those markets.

Which emerging market interests you the most? What moats have you seen most often in that market?

Probably Indonesia. It has some real corruption problems, but there are delightful businesses based there that are growing at an extremely rapid pace. This might sound weird, but I also appreciate Saudi Arabia as a market.

What's your favorite country to travel to and invest in?

(Try not to say Indonesia again, but Bali......wow.) South Africa is an interesting market and an absolutely, positively unbelievable place to travel. I stay away from mining and natural resources companies, simply because their costs of capital are high and they tend to have very few moats or pricing advantages. But South Africa is the largest economy and the driving force in Africa, a continent with   1.2 billion people in it.

I have been involved with a group called the Fistula Foundation which has taken me to many places in Africa. The Fistula Foundation helps women get access to surgeries for an easily correctable complication that comes during childbirth. Perhaps because it's such an emotional thing to see these women literally get their lives back, I have a really deep connection to the time I've spent in Ethiopia, Kenya, and Malawi and would return in a second.

This conversation has sparked my interest, and hopefully for others, in external markets, and I cannot wait to explore that! I learned a lot and there is so much more to learn. Because I am extremely new to investing in markets outside of the U.S., I will simply quote the famous Charlie Munger says, "I have nothing to add."

Metrics

*"The stock market is filled with individuals who know
the price of everything, but the value of nothing."*
–Phillip Fisher

Investing can be thought of as long term or short term
commitments. True investing is for the long term, and
only the long term. Speculators focus on short term; I
invest for the long term. The money you invest with
should be strictly for future purposes, like college funds
or getting started with your independent life after
college. Because investing is for the long term (I cannot
say this enough), you will not get to take that money out
of the stock for around 10 years or whenever you choose
to sell. Therefore, patience is the key.

The question many people ask is, how do I know if a
company is worth buying? First, you want to find a
company you are interested in. How do you do that? Just
look around at things you are in contact with daily. Is
there something that a lot of people buy and use every
day? Look around your kitchen. What do you see?
Maybe soup, mayonnaise, peanut butter, coffee, and
orange juice? What about the napkins and paper towels?
What about dishwasher detergent? What companies
make these?

Next, do you think they will still buy, use or need those
products or services in 5-10 years?

Some types of food, paper products, and cleaning
products will continue to be a stable purchase for people

for a very long time; that's what makes it a safe investment. This is why I don't recommend teenage trends or clothing lines because they are popular but only for short amounts of time. Instead, you want to invest in something that has and can withstand the test of time.

Consumer staples are a great place to start. Consumer staples are a range of products that can be found in your kitchen or bathroom. Think toothpaste and shampoo. They may seem like the most boring companies in the world, but if they do, then you are probably on the right track. Boring is a great way to make money as an investor. These are some examples of companies with Consumer staples products.

Consumer Staples Companies	Product Examples
Procter & Gamble	Tide, Pampers, Gillette, Olay, Duracell, Bounty, etc.
General Mills	Cheerios, Cocoa Puffs, Chex, Yoplait, Betty Crocker, Nature Valley, etc.
Unilever	Axe, Lipton Tea, Skippy's Peanut Butter, Vaseline, Dove, etc.
JM Smucker	Smucker's Peanut Butter, Smucker's Jelly, Crisco, etc.
Hormel	Spam, Canned Beans, Bacon, Pepperoni Sticks, etc.
Pepsi	Pepsi Soda, Lays Chips, Quaker Oats, Mountain Dew, etc.
McCormick	Spices of all sorts: Paprika, Garlic Salt, Black Pepper, etc.

Once you find a company or two, then you have to ask yourself if you think the company is on the right track. Do you believe they can continue to grow with that idea without a high possibility of having problems from strong competitors?

Find things you are familiar with. Recently, an eighth grader asked me to help him to start investing. The first thing I told him to do was to find companies he was interested in. He came back with a list of about 20 companies. There was a large range of stocks from Johnson & Johnson (JNJ) to Nike (NKE). These are both good companies because they have been successful and profitable over many years. Next, I will show you how you can research the numbers that show if they have a successful history.

Metrics You Need

After you make a list of companies that you are interested in and that have a competitive advantage, you have to find a way to research them at a deeper level. I am going to use the company Johnson & Johnson (JNJ) as my example. Johnson & Johnson is a pharmaceutical and consumer healthcare company that sells products like Band-Aids, shampoo, conditioner, etc.

The first step to researching a company is to find their ticker symbol. All you have to do for that is look up on Google Finance to see if that company is publicly traded. If so, normally a chart will show up and you can find the ticker symbol right next to the company's name.

From there, I use Morningstar [11] to research the financial metrics. To do that you want to go to Morningstar and search the ticker symbol in the quote box.

---

[11] www.morningstar.com/

71

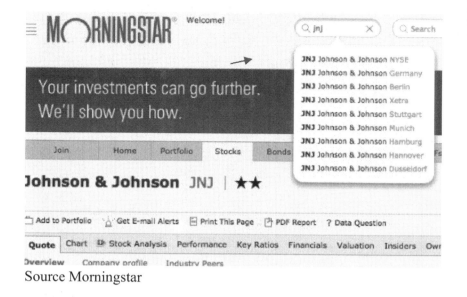

Source Morningstar

Once I get to the company page I want to find the important metrics. I want to look for these numbers;

- <u>Price to Earnings Ratio</u> (P/E): 20 or lower
- <u>Dividend</u> (Yield): 2% to 5%
- <u>Debt</u>: 1.0 or lower
- Return on Equity (ROE): 15% or higher
- <u>Gross Margin</u>.: 25% or higher

I will go into depth on each of these metrics after we learn how to find them.

See dividend yield
Source Morningstar

Once I've found the metrics, I need to check if it meets my requirements. My Dividend/Yield requirement is 2-5%. A dividend is a percentage of earnings that they give to you. Johnson & Johnson's is 2.6%, so it meets the requirement. Next, you want to scroll down the page to find a table called Key Stats.

Key Stats JNJ   More...

	Stock	Ind Avg	Relative to Industry
Price/Earnings TTM	21.5	26.8	
Price/Book	4.6	4.0	
Price/Sales TTM	4.8	3.9	
Rev Growth (3 Yr Avg)	1.4	-5.1	
Net Income Growth (3 Yr Avg)	12.4	-14.3	
Operating Margin % TTM	27.5	19.4	
Net Margin % TTM	22.3	14.3	
ROA TTM	11.7	5.9	
ROE TTM	22.1	15.5	
Debt/Equity	0.3	0.6	

See Price to Earnings, ROE, and Debt
Source Morningstar

Then, we want to look at Price to Earnings Ratio (P/E Ratio). P/E is comparing the price of the company to the share price to the earnings the company makes. For P/E my requirement is 20 or under. Johnson & Johnson's P/E Ratio is slightly over my requirement at 21.5, but not too much to worry.

Next is ROE. Return on Equity measures the profitability of a company. My ROE requirement is 15% or higher. It's at 22.1 so it does meet that requirement.

Last but not least is debt. That should ideally be under 1.0. This is a metric that you should be especially worried about if it is too high. Sometimes a company's debt can be justified by things such as buying another company, building a factory, etc. This metric is one that you should definitely look into on the investment service of your choice.

Lastly, at the top of the page there are multiple small tabs. Currently, you should be on the one that says "Quote." If you click "Key Ratios" you will be able to find Gross Margin. Now that we know how to find them let's learn what they are.

Price/Earnings Ratio

As an investor, you look at the value of the company. The company's value is based on their Earnings. Earnings are how much money the company makes.

The first thing you need to know about P/E Ratios is what P and E stand for. P stands for Price and E for Earnings; therefore, Price divided by Earnings. A P/E Ratio calculates how much you will have to pay to get a dollar of the company's earnings. If Mattel's(MAT) P/E Ratio is 31.3 that would mean when you pay $31.30 you would get a dollar of Mattel's earnings. A Price to Earnings Ratio is there to show you how much you, as an investor, have to pay to earn a dollar of the company's earnings.

Here's how to calculate it. First, you need to find the Earnings per Share. That is located on the Key Ratios page (I use Morningstar[12] for my stock research[13]).

---

[12] www.morningstar.com/

Mattel's Earnings per share is $1.02 and their Price per share (the price for one share of Mattel stock) is $31.97. You should be able to find that on the page titled Quote.

When you divide the two numbers, 31.97/1.02, you get 31.3. That would be their P/E Ratio. As a stockholder, you want the lowest P/E Ratio. The reason you want the smallest P/E Ratio possible is so you pay the smallest amount to get a dollar of the company's earnings. Although this is one of the simpler metrics it is very important and can be hard to understand. The price of the share does not matter, what matters is the earnings that you receive as part owner of the company.

If we look at Hasbro and Mattel, they both do similar things but their P/E Ratios are so different. Mattel's, as we know, is 31.30 and Hasbro's is 21. When you look at the prices, Mattel's seems like a much better deal, $31.97 versus $80.16, but when you dig deeper, you can tell that to pay only $21 you get a dollar of Hasbro's earnings, whereas you have to pay $31.30 to get a dollar of Mattel's.

---

[13] On the Quote page of <u>Morningstar</u> they show the forward P/E, that is different than the current P/E. Forward P/E is the predicted P/E for the company in the next year coming up, and the P/E is the current P/E for the last twelve months. We want to use the current P/E. Mattel for example has a forward P/E of 17.5 and a current P/E of 31.3. Not only are the numbers different, but what they are showing. As most predictions are, the forward P/E Ratio is a guess. The CEO/CFO is guessing what their earnings will be which will affect their stock price which will then affect their P/E Ratio. All in all it's a big guessing game, some years it could be right and other maybe not. That is why the current P/E Ratio is more reliable, it is all the information that they have making it true.

Companies	P/E Ratio
Mattel	31.30
Hasbro (Winner-lower P/E Ratio)	21

Source Morningstar

Last but not least, we will use a lemonade story to go over the calculations in a simpler way. Lily and Sara started a lemonade stand, and sold four shares of their business at $2 apiece to four family members. That day they made a profit of $1.60 selling lemonade.

Lily and Sara were waiting for their customers when their mother, Kristin ran over.

"Girls," she said, "all my friends have been asking me what the price to earnings ratio is for your lemonade stand and I don't know how to calculate it."

"Mom, we learned this ages ago," said Sara.

"You take the price of the share, in our case it's $2.00, and divide that by our earnings per share, which is $0.40. That would give you five." Lily said.

"Five what?" asked their confused mother.

"Just five," Sara said, "It's a ratio, not a percentage, nor is it a amount of money."

"Thank you, girls. Now I know what to tell my friends!"

P/E Ratios change as does the information that you need to calculate the Ratio. Like other metrics for stocks you want to watch it and sell at a high and buy at a low.

Profit Margins

This section will take you step by step on how to calculate the Profit Margins of any company you have an interest in. A Profit Margin is how much money the company gets to keep as a profit out of the total amount they spent. Sources such as Morningstar[14] and Motley Fool[15] help you find the exact calculations without doing the research but you should at least know how to find the data you need and how to calculate it. As an investor, it's important to know why I'm even talking about this. Well, it's because the money or the profit that the company makes determines how much the investors will get.

There are many kinds of Profit Margins. The most common one is called Net Profit Margins. First, we are going to look at a big picture idea, showing Lily and Sara's Lemonade Stand's Profit Margins. Next, we are going to look at NPM (Net Profit Margins) for real companies, Walmart and Johnson & Johnson.

Lily and Sara are selling their lemonade for $0.50 a cup. Farhang, their father, bought $8.00 worth of cups, sugar and lemons for the two girls to start their lemonade stand. If they sold $10.00 worth of lemonade, and had to

---

[14] www.morningstar.com/
[15] www.fool.com

pay $8.00 back to Farhang, what is their Profit Margin?

Let's calculate together. If they spent $8.00 on the ingredients and subtracted that from the amount they sold, $10.00, they would get $2.00 of profit. Then you would divide $2.00 by $10.00 which would give you 1/5, otherwise known as 20%. When the girls sell $10.00 worth of lemonade, they would have a 20% Profit Margin.

$10.00(revenue) - $8.00(cost of ingredients) = $2.00(profit)

Now on to NPM (Net Profit Margins). It's an easy but very helpful tool. Let's first learn how to calculate it and then look at some examples. To calculate Net Profit Margins, you need to know a few vocabulary words. *Net income*: Net Income is the profit that the company makes. In the lemonade stand example, the girls Net Income was $2.00. *Revenue*: Not the same thing as income. Revenue is all the money that the company earns. Lily and Sara's Revenue is all the $10.00, profit and all.

We explained how to calculate income, but as a recap you take how much you made in earnings and subtract that from the total cost of the items you needed to buy to make the company's product. For example, when Farhang paid for Lily and Sara's lemonade stand, he had to buy all the ingredients so they could make their lemonade. It ended up having a total cost of $8.00. To calculate NPM, you have to complete two steps:

1) Find the Net Income.

2) Divide the Net Income by the Revenue, which brings us to your total percentage of Net Profit Margins.

It's important to know three things:

1) When you divide the Net Income by the Revenue, it means that the Net Income goes into the Revenue.
2) When you're looking at stocks to invest in, you want to check the difference between the NPM of the company compared to the Industry Average. Preferably, the company's NPM is higher than the Industry average.
3) You can find the industry average of most metrics next to the metric you are looking at. For all the examples in this chapter, I am using the data source Morningstar[16].

I am going to use Johnson & Johnson versus Walmart. We have already talked about Johnson & Johnson, but for those who don't know, Walmart is a chain store that sells groceries, school supplies, golf clubs, and much more.

---

[16] www.morningstar.com/

Johnson & Johnson JNJ | ★★

Statement Type	Data Type	Period
Annual ▼	As of Reported ▼	5 Years

Fiscal year ends in December
USD in Million except per share data

		TTM
Revenue	�|..⅃	70,877
Cost of revenue	⅃|..⅃	21,562
Gross profit	⅃|..⅃	49,315
▼ Operating expenses		
Research and developme...	⅃|..⅃	9,295
Sales, General and adm...	⅃|..⅃	20,836
Other operating expens...	⅃|..⅃	253
Total operating expens...	⅃|..⅃	**30,384**
Operating income	⅃|..⅃	18,931
Interest Expense	⅃|..⅃	633
Other income (expense)	⅃|..⅃	(220)
Income before taxes	⅃|..⅃	18,078
Provision for income t...	⅃|..⅃	3,051
Net income from contin...	⅃|..⅃	15,027

When you look on your preferred investment service (remember, Motley Fool or Morningstar are two options) to find the data for a stock, you want to look for two things, the Net Income and Revenue. First, we will look at Johnson & Johnson (JNJ). Their Revenue for 2016 is $70.8 billion and their Net Income is $15 billion. Now what we want to do is divide $15 billion by $70.8 billion. That gives us an NPM of 21%, meaning for every dollar Johnson & Johnson makes for Revenue the company earns $0.21.

Wal-Mart Stores Inc WMT | ★

Add to Portfolio   Get E-mail Alerts   Print This Page

Quote   Chart   Stock Analysis   Performance   Key Rati

Income Statement   Balance Sheet   Cash Flow

Statement Type	Data Type	Period
Annual	As of Reported	5 Years

Fiscal year ends in January
USD in Million except per share data

		TTM
Revenue		483,208
Cost of revenue		361,045
Gross profit		122,163
▼ Operating expenses		
Sales, General and adm...		98,463
Total operating expens...		**98,463**
Operating income		23,700
Interest Expense		2,290
Other income (expense)		86
Income before income t...		21,496
Provision for income t...		6,483
Minority interest		581
Other income		581
Net income from contin...		15,013

If we look at Walmart they have a Revenue for 2016 of $483 million and a Net Income of $15 million. When we do the division that would give us 3%, meaning, again, for every dollar they make as Revenue they keep $0.03.

$15,013 (Net Income)/$483,208 (Revenue) = 3%

If I spend $100 at Walmart, Walmart makes about $3.00 after its own costs, which means as a consumer, they are giving us cheap products. If I bought $100 of Johnson & Johnson products, they would make $21.00. Walmart may look like a bad stock for short term investing, but look at the long run.

Dividend Reinvestment Calculator updated Aug 13, 2016

International Exchange Codes

Stock Symbol:	WMT
Select Start Date:	Aug 25 1972
Select End Date:	Aug 12 2016
Annualized Return:	18.60%
$ 1000 Is Worth:	$1,819,412.96
Earliest Date Found:	August 25, 1972

Calculate Return

If we look at the returns to investors from Walmart's long run compounding, we see after 44 years they turned a starting investment of $1,000 into over $1 million. I used Long Run Data[17], a website that tracks the past growth of any selected company, to find this information.

---

[17] www.longrundata.com/

Johnson & Johnson didn't do so badly either over the same 44 years.

What these examples show is that companies with earnings over the long run can make a lot of money for their investors.

It's also important to see if the company's Profit Margins are increasing or decreasing. Let's look at the past five years. As you can see, they both were pretty consistent. Over five years, Johnson & Johnson went up six percentage points compared to Walmart's zero.

Dividend Reinvestment Calculator updated Aug 13, 2016

International Exchange Codes

Stock Symbol:	JNJ
Select Start Date:	Aug ⌃ 25 ⌃ 1972 ⌃
Select End Date:	Aug ⌃ 12 ⌃ 2016 ⌃
Annualized Return:	11.59%
$ 1000 Is Worth:	$124,352.35
Earliest Date Found:	June 15, 1970

Calculate Return

Profit Margin Comparison

Companies	2012	2013	2014	2015	2016
Johnson & Johnson	15%	19%	21%	21%	21%
Walmart	3%	3%	3%	3%	3%

Source: Morningstar

Dividend

Dividends are very important to compounding. They are a cash payment you get quarterly or annually, depending on the company. When I first learned about Dividends, I only cared about two things, when I would get paid and how much. I can give you answer to both. You *usually* get paid four times a year, every quarter or once every three months. To figure out how much, let's use another lemonade story.

Farhang and his wife Kristin are both shareholders of the lemonade stand. Lily and Sara created four shares. Each member of the family owns a quarter of the lemonade stand.

Kristin wants to know, after investing, how much will she get as a dividend? Lily and Sara tell their mother that they will pay 40% of their earnings as a dividend, meaning each shareholder will get 10% of their profits. Farhang was confused by this metric, so he asked his daughters to explain their reasoning.

"There are four shares sold. To become a shareholder,

you have to pay $2.00 per share," Lily explained.

"We decided that we want to pay 40% of our earnings back to you. If we earn $2.00, our profits, and took 40% of that, it would come to $0.80 total," Sara added.

Lily chimed in and said, "Then we had to divide the number of shares we have, four, by the total number of dividends paid, $0.80, which would give us a $0.20 dividend. If you divide $0.20 by $2.00 you get 10%, which is your dividend."

Later in the lemonade season, Farhang was grateful for his daughters' explanation and enjoyed his $0.20 dividend.

Here are a few important things to know about Dividends:

1. Companies try to pay their shareholders Dividends in tough times. This sounds nice, but it is a little troubling because Dividends are paid from the company's profits. If the company doesn't make enough money and is still are committed to paying they get into to serious problems with debt.

2. Most small companies don't pay Dividends because it's too much of a risk or they want to use the money to grow. It sounds like a big deal, and it is, but there are other ways to make money. The easiest way is when a stock goes up.

If Elise owns a small store that has local customers that come every Monday and Friday, but then a new Whole

Foods with cheaper prices is built across the street, no matter how loyal you think the customers are, if Whole Foods has better prices, they will cross to the other side of the street. Now Elise is stuck. She has to pay her shareholder's Dividends off of her decreased profit. She has a smaller set of customers that visit her store, rather than her previous steady income of all of the locals. That's one reason why most small companies don't pay Dividends. If you look at the market and there aren't a lot of large businesses, the market is mostly made up of small companies.

3. Many large companies do pay a Dividend. They are more stable and more developed as a whole. That said, it's still a risk, but it depends on the company. Always do your own research and figure out what you're comfortable with. Johnson & Johnson for example has grown their Dividends every year for 53 years.

4. It's important to know how much of the company's profits are spent on Dividends. This metric is called the Dividend Payout Ratio or Payout Ratio. First, we will learn how to calculate it and then what it is and why it's important.

Johnson & Johnson JNJ

Quote   Chart Stock Analysis   Performanc

Financials

	TTM
Revenue USD Mil	70,877
Gross Margin %	69.6
Operating Income USD Mil	18,931
Operating Margin %	26.7
Net Income USD Mil	15,027
Earnings Per Share USD	5.37
Dividends USD	3.05
Payout Ratio %	56.8

See Payout Ratio %
Source Morningstar

If Josie wanted to invest in Johnson & Johnson, she would want to know how much of their profits they spent paying their shareholders. As you can see the Payout Ratio is 56.8%. That means over half of their profits are spent on Dividends. As an investor, you have to decide for yourself what's too risky. Johnson & Johnson is a very successful company and has had a higher Payout Ratio. It hasn't seemed to affect them yet, but I would watch the Ratio very carefully to make sure it doesn't get too high.

Debt

Debt is one of the most important parts of investing. People can get hung up on how much or little Debt the company has, but it's always important to dig deeper. Sometimes there is an important reason that they have that Debt. The company could be opening new stores or launching a new website. For the people who like rules, I want to stress that you that you need to set your own comfortable boundaries. Some people are comfortable with more Debt. It depends on whether you don't mind taking a risk or if you are a stay in the boat type of person.

When you hear the horror stories about companies closing down or when you walk by your favorite local restaurant that has abruptly shut down, most of the time it's because of Debt. Yes, sometimes if it's a restaurant it might not be up to code, which could be because they couldn't afford it. Why couldn't they afford it? Because of Debt. Forbes[18] says 8 out of 10 businesses fail because of lack of cash, otherwise known as Debt.

We all cringe when we hear the word Debt. Even as a child I think I did. Debt can show how well the company is managing their money. The money that is invested into a company isn't your mom's money, no, *it's your money* and if the company messes up, then it's your

---

[18] www.forbes.com/

money on the line. Debt causes bankruptcy. You lose your business and have to start everything from scratch if you choose to start again.

I am making Debt sound like a horrible thing, but it's not always. Here are two examples of how Debt can either make or break your company.

Sara and Lily want to try to sell more lemonade than they did the first time. They ask their dad, Farhang to invest $16.00 in the lemonade stand, instead of the normal $8.00. After selling $8.00 worth of lemonade it starts to rain. Lily and Sara have to close their stand and go inside. They pay Farhang back $8 of his $16. Because they lack the other half of his money, Lily and Sara now have $8.00 Debt. They did make the $8.00 in the next lemonade stand but due to the rain it took them a while to pay Farhang back. If Lily and Sara were dealing with a bank for loan along with the $8.00 they would have to pay interest.

That's one way to look at Debt. Now let's look at the other.

Lily and Sara feel like they did so well with the one lemonade stand that they wanted to invest in more stands. They had to pay for two tables, $60.00; triple the cost of the ingredients, $24.00; and one quarter of the Profit. Because they only make $2.00 per lemonade stand, they will be $84.00 in Debt.

Both stories cause Debt but one will be easier to work out of than the other. In the first story, because of an unexpected problem, Lily and Sara lost money. It wasn't their fault that they lost money. It was just something they didn't prepare for. If Lily and Sara's stand has too many slipups like that, Farhang won't invest in their stand anymore because he will be unsure if he'll get his money back.

In the second story, Lily and Sara decided to invest in two more lemonade stands that caused more Debt in the beginning but if they are as successful as the first stand they will soon pay it off.

	Number of stands	Amount of Debt	Earnings	Amount of Debt Left
Three Stands Scenario	3	$84.00	$6.00	-$78.00
One Stand Scenario	1	$8.00	$2.00	-$6.00

***$2 per stand

As you can see, it can make sense to acquire Debt in some cases. Sometimes you need to in order for your business to grow. Now let's look at how to measure Debt.

It's hard to see but the metric we want is the Market
Cap.

Source: Morningstar

It's important to know how to calculate and use the Debt
to Equity Ratio. Let's look at the stock AmeriGas.
AmeriGas is a propane provider. Debt is how much
money they still owe, and Equity is the value of the
company, otherwise known as the Market Cap.

We need to find the Debt to Equity Ratio. The website
Morningstar[19] gives us the Debt to Equity Ratio which is
2.0.

That is how much AmeriGas has in Debt, two dollars of
debt for every one dollar of company market value. The
company uses some debt to buy trucks and propane
tanks. Whether this is a good use of debt or not is what
investors need to figure out for themselves. Again,
depending on how risky of an investor you are, this
might be too much Debt.

---

[19] www.morningstar.com/

Another important thing investors should know about is Interest Coverage. On Morningstar[20], you can find it at the bottom of the Key Ratios page. Interest Coverage is a ratio that shows how many years the company could pay its interest Debt. Higher is better in this case. Let's say that my cousin's company, Mini Foods Inc. owes me $100. I decide to give her 10% interest. That means she owes me $10 for the first year's interest payment. Her company earns $130 per year, so with $130 of earnings, versus $10 of interest, her Interest Coverage ratio is 13. That means that she can pay the annual 10% interest for 13 years from this year's earnings.

Hopefully that makes a little more sense, so let's look at another example. For a stock, you have to find the pretax earnings and then add the interest expense. That will give you the EBIT, or the Earnings Before Interest and Taxes. After that you have to divide the EBIT by the interest expense and that will tell give you the answer to the ratio. Now we'll look at a real-life example.

---

[20] www.morningstar.com/

Mattel Inc MAT | ★★

Add to Portfolio   Get E-mail Alerts   Print This Page   PDF Report

Quote   Chart   ▣ Stock Analysis   Performance   Key Ratios   **Financ**

Income Statement   Balance Sheet   Cash Flow

Statement Type	Data Type	Period	
Annual ▾	As of Reported ▾	5 Years	▾

Fiscal year ends in December
USD in Million except per share data

		TTM
Revenue		5,618
Cost of revenue		2,913
Gross profit		2,705
▼ Operating expenses		
Sales, General and adm...		2,171
Total operating expens...		**2,171**
Operating income		534
Interest Expense		89
Other income (expense)		(11)
Income before taxes		434
Provision for income t...		87
Net income from contin...		347
Net income		347

Source: Morningstar

Let's look at Mattel. Their pretax earnings are $347 million so we want to add that to $89 million, for an answer of $436 million. That means that the EBIT is $436 million. Next, we will divide the EBIT by $89 million, the interest expense. The answer is 5. That

means just from this year's profit, Mattel can pay five
years' worth of their Debt.

SUPERVALU Inc SVU

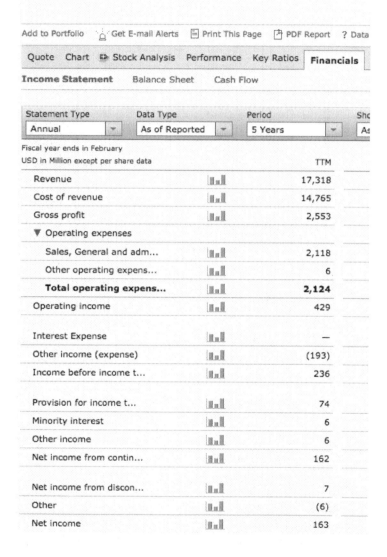

| Quote   Chart   Stock Analysis   Performance   Key Ratios | **Financials** |

Income Statement   Balance Sheet   Cash Flow

Statement Type	Data Type	Period	Sho
Annual	As of Reported	5 Years	As

Fiscal year ends in February
USD in Million except per share data

		TTM
Revenue		17,318
Cost of revenue		14,765
Gross profit		2,553
▼ Operating expenses		
Sales, General and adm...		2,118
Other operating expens...		6
Total operating expens...		**2,124**
Operating income		429
Interest Expense		—
Other income (expense)		(193)
Income before income t...		236
Provision for income t...		74
Minority interest		6
Other income		6
Net income from contin...		162
Net income from discon...		7
Other		(6)
Net income		163

Source: Morningstar

It's always good to add in an example of what not to look for. Even for risky investors, this stock is a no-go. We are going to look at a company called SuperValu, a grocery store that got itself into a predicament. They are having a bankruptcy problem, so they don't have an Interest Expense. That means the data I'll be using is from 2015. Their pretax earnings are $192 million next we add that to $244 million, that gives us $436 million. Now we divide that by $244 million. The Interest Coverage Ratio is 2 (Please note that it's rounded. The exact answer is 1.7). It's funny that Mattel and SuperValu had the same EBIT, but their Interest Coverage Ratio is very different. Both earn the same, but Mattel investors get more earnings and have to make way less debt payments.

The last question about Debt is "Why should investors care?" I found a great conversation an investor had with Tom Gayner about Mr. Gayner's opinion on companies with Debt. If it's confusing to follow, read my summary. This helps you better understand why Debt is dangerous and quite important to pay attention to.

"If you're looking to buy businesses, don't buy businesses where they use a lot of Debt. And I wondered why.

And he said, well, if you want to make sure that you're dealing with high-quality, high-integrity people, generally speaking, high-quality, high-integrity people don't use a lot of Debt or not so much that, but if you're a bad person, if you were sort of a little bit of a crook or had a little bit of larceny in your heart, it's unlikely that you would use 100% equity finance. Because when it's equity financed it means it's your own money. When it's Debt, you're running your business on other people's money.

He says crooks don't steal their own money, they steal other people's money. So when you see a business that sort of relies on a bunch of Debt to operate and be successful, that adds a layer of concern or diligence that you have to do, you have to think about, that you don't have to do if you look at a business that just doesn't use much Debt. So it's a margin of safety. That's a word and a phrase that Ben Graham used quite a bit in thinking about investing, by looking at companies that don't use much Debt. That really protects your downside and protects you from bad things happening."

Summary:

Tom Gayner believes that companies with high debt are risky. He believes that the type of people that acquire large amounts of debt can be simply thought of as crooks. Crooks steal other people's money, they don't take it from themselves, that makes it easier to continually increase the company's debt. This does not mean that everyone or every company with high debt are crooks; as we talked about before, the story is very important to connect to the numbers, but in his example, he explains that crooks don't use their own money, they use others.

Don't Forget!
- The main metrics to use are:
  - Price to Earnings Ratio: 20 or lower
  - Yield (Dividend): 2% to 5%
  - Return on Equity: 15% or higher
  - Profit Margins: 25% or higher
  - Debt: Under 1.0

The Power of Compounding

"All you need for a lifetime of successful investing is a few big winners, and the pluses from those will overwhelm the minuses from the stocks that don't work out." -Peter Lynch

Compounding is an investing style. It's something I'll commonly refer to as a "snowball." Just as a snowball rolls down a hill and slowly collects more snow, increasing its size, so do long held investments grow in value throughout time.

A simple estimate for figuring out how long it will take for the money you invested in a stock to double is The Rule of 72. Unlike other investing rules, you can easily find the amount of time it will take to double in value just by having the rate of return.

Let's say Ginnie wants to invest in Smarticles Inc. She has done all the research and checked all the boxes on the debt and value, but she still has one more question, "How long will it take for me to double my money in Smarticles Inc.?" Ginnie pulls out her handy-dandy newspaper and researches to calculate her growth rate, which she figures to be at about 8%. To find her final estimate of how long her money will take to double, Ginnie has to take the number 72 and divide that by the company's rate of return, 8%. That will give her a total of nine years.

Please note, this rule does not give you the exact answer. For the exact number of years, it will take you to double your money you can find a <u>calculator online</u>[21].

Remember dividends? One way to speed up doubling your money is by reinvesting your dividends. Reinvesting dividends puts more money into your stocks, or adding shares. If you think of it that way, it will obviously mean a faster increase. Two people may buy the same stock. They might get the same amount of shares, but what will happen if one reinvests their dividends and the other doesn't? That is what we are about to look at.

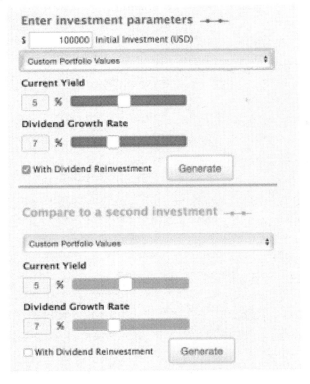

---

[21] www.sugar.mhinvest.com/YOI/investment.php

Yield on Original Investment (YOI)

Click to view Compounding of Shares

If you look at the picture above, you will notice that there are two lines. They have the same dividend growth rate, 7%, and the same current yield, 5%. For some reason, we see a very large difference in how the dividend is growing. Why? The blue line is reinvesting dividends and the orange one isn't.

Let's look at an example of how this might play out. Pretend the blue line belongs to Jackie. Jackie is 10 years old and bought $100,000 in Smarticles Inc. stock. Yes, I know that is a lot of money for a 10-year-old to have, but let's pretend she has been very successful in the lemonade business. Because Jackie is so young, she isn't in a rush to acquire and spend her dividends. Actually, it would be more profitable for her to keep reinvesting until she needs the money or the stock isn't performing the way she wants it to.

Jill is much older than Jackie and she's retired. Jill bought the same stock as Jackie did. It has the same yield, the same growth rate, and she also paid $100,000 for the stock. The difference is that Jill has no other income. She is living off of the dividend that Smarticles is giving her so she can't reinvest it.

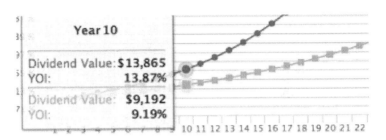

10 Years Later.

If we refer to the image above you can see that at year 10, the blue line, Jackie, has more than doubled her starting $5,000 of dividends. Jill's money has compounded and grown but there is still more to go if she wants to double her money.

When Jill and Jackie first invested in the stock there was no difference. Now that one chose to reinvest dividends and the other didn't there is a difference of $4,673 of dividends. In year 20 of owning Smarticles Inc. they will have a difference of $24,981. By looking at the differences of the two owners you can see how much the stock has compounded and grown. Jackie invested in Smarticles when she was 10, if she continues hold it for 20 years she would get $43,064 of dividend. And that is the power of compounding and reinvesting dividends.

	Jackie Reinvested Dividends	Jackie YOI	Jill Did Not Reinvest Dividends	Jill YOI
Original investment	$5,000	5%	$5,000	5%
Year 5	$7,868	7.87%	$6,554	6.55%
Year 10	$13,865	13.87%	$9,192	9.19%
Year 15	$24,436	24.44%	$12,893	12.89%
Year 20	$43,064	43.06%	$18,083	18.08%

***YOI stands for Yield on Original Investment. ***

Reinvesting dividends is like having the perfect snow for a snowball and finding that ideal long hill.

Don't Forget!
- Reinvesting dividends is very powerful.
- Being patient and having time will work in your favor.

The People of the Investing World

"I will tell you how to become rich. Close the doors. Be fearful when others are greedy. Be greedy when others are fearful." -Warren Buffett

David Gardner

I recently talked to David Gardner, one of the founders of The Motley Fool[22]. In 1993, he started an investment newsletter geared toward families in an effort to get more people, of all ages, to invest. David Gardner is an intelligent, Foolish, out of the box thinker. His approach to investing is light and fun, as is shown in The Motley Fool's mission, *"To Educate, To Amuse and To Enrich."* As Gardner says, "It's that middle phrase that is surprising to people." Most people don't think of a financial publishing company as an entertainment center, but there is more to investing than putting money into a stock and waiting. I have a few main takeaways I would like to share with you from our talk.

Investing Mentality

I've said it, and David Gardner has said it: investing is a mentality. When you become a part owner, you become engulfed in the company. Investing is about much more than money, David Gardner says, "The word invest comes from the Latin word *investire* which means 'to put on the clothes of.' If you know the word *vestments*

---

[22] www.fool.com/

it's the same thing. So, the word, the root of the word, the initial meaning was that. Just looking deeply inside that word, I didn't see anything about money."

Investing yourself in something is immersing yourself. When you buy shares of a company, you are immersing yourself, you are investing yourself into that company. When you do that, you are buying into three main things, the company's goals and beliefs, their marketplace, and their people.

Becoming a Fan of Your Company

From there, Mr. Gardner went into an analogy, "Good investing is kind of like a sports fan... They are going to be a fan whether their team wins or loses that day. [Good investors are not] going to sell their stock whether or not it goes up or down, today, this week or even this year because they're in it to win it over the only term that counts, which is the long term." I don't think I could've said it any better. When your team makes a mistake, you stick with them. Just because the Red Sox lose a game or two doesn't mean you are suddenly a Yankees fan.

A company's overall reputation and returns is determined by the long term. In the short term, they can make mistakes but it's how they recover that shines through. It's the same with sports teams. Gardner says of investing, "That word, by definition, means long term."

Why People Aren't Investing

David Gardner says, "The biggest reason people are not investing is because they don't understand or know about it... We have done different things over the course of the last 20 years [at The Motley Fool] trying to reach people of all ages and get them to invest and to save... It's not a problem of lack of effort on our part, it's actually I think that there is not enough of a culture of awareness among people of all ages that there even is a stock market or that you could be a part owner of a company."

The Motley Fool is trying to get everyone's attention with their lighthearted investing style and new "trendy" ideas to create a culture of awareness. Along with creating classes to present to schools around DC called Fool School, they are developing a new video game involving the stock market. Over the past 20 years, they have been very successful at reaching out to more and more people around the world, but there is still a lot more to do.

To finish this, let's talk about how to get people to invest. David Gardner puts it simply, "By engaging them and getting their attention, we need to maybe ask the Socratic dialogue question. We need to ask them a question that they themselves realize they should know the answer, but they don't. And it causes them to begin asking their own questions and finding out some new answers. A phrase I like a lot, 'switching on.'"

Switching on requires people to think about their future selves and what will benefit them in the long run. The only constant in our lives is change. We need to switch people on to think about changes for 10 years from now and beyond. That is hard "because of the ease of remembering versus the difficulty of imagining," says Dan Gilbert[23].

I'll leave you with a few questions.

Why don't people invest? And why not start sooner?

Are there other alternatives to investing that are more appealing?

What do people have to sacrifice to invest? (The best time to plant a tree was 20 years ago. The second-best time is now.)

Why is investing a good option to make money in the long term?

---

[23]www.ted.com/talks/dan_gilbert_you_are_a

Aunt Ginny

 Ginny is an 90-year-old woman. She has a passion for investing, math and numbers. We talked for hours about our mutual passion over tea and cookies and I learned five critical things from our conversation that I would like to share with you. She taught about how successful simple companies can be, what it was like to be a woman investor in the 1960s, and what time can do for an investor. I hope you enjoy her story as much as I did.

Success with Simplicity

Ginny lives in a small town in Minnesota and has been investing for many years. As a wedding gift from her father-in-law, Ginny and her husband received shares of stock. She decided she had better learn about investing. That one gift fired her lifelong passion in investing. She slowly learned more and more until it became her main interest. Once she got started, she never stopped.

While Ginny and her young family were on a road trip, they stopped for breakfast at a pancake diner. Time and again on this trip they ran into the same chain. Each diner had one thing in common, they all had overflowing parking lots! After her curiosity bubbled for a few states, she asked the waitress if she knew who owned this chain. It was Quaker Oats. When Ginny returned home, she bought many shares of the stock. Later, Pepsi bought Quaker Oats and that is how she came to own Pepsi. Ginny invested in something she was curious about, that she was a customer of, and that she understood. Slowly, with time, it became something much bigger than that.

In her later years of investing, she bought Valspar, which we know now as Sherwin Williams. She bought Valspar because she walked into her friend's house and immediately fell in love with her walls. Yes, of course after falling in love with those walls, she did a lot of research. All you need is a stock that you understand, to believe in what the company does, and a lot of research.

More recently, Ginny bought an oxygen company. As a 90-year-old woman she saw that many of her friends were on oxygen. This is a good example of noticing the world around you and investing in what you know.

Even with a long history of investing, Ginny has decided to stick with the companies she is familiar with. She is a great example of how investing should be viewed. Ginny found things she knew about and loved, paint color and pancakes, and checked their numbers. Investing may seem like a gamble, but it really comes down to investing in what you know and making sure the company meets the requirements you want it to.

Stocks and Scones

When I visited Ginny last fall, our conversation started out with deciding what tea we wanted. We talked about everything from flowers to fridges to investing. Ginny is a thoughtful, welcoming, and very down-to-earth woman with many good investing tips and ideas. She is the real deal when it comes to investing; she just wears a smart blue sweater, instead of a three-piece suit, and her corner office is her dining room table with a sweeping view of the river.

My favorite part of our meeting was when I walked in the door and instead of interviewing her, she started interviewing me. She asked what stocks I owned. I listed a few and when I got to some of my prouder holdings, Pepsi, her face brightened and she quickly, loudly stated, "I beat you on Pepsi, I beat you on Pepsi!" She made it very clear who the investing queen was. She proceeded to tell me she was no genius, and not a mathematician; she looked at the numbers and watched the people.

After doing a thorough analysis of the stock, Ginny can normally tell you if that stock is a keeper or not. She made it very clear that there is no trick to investing. You just need to invest in what you know, whether that is a toy company or everyday things that you find in your daily life. She writes everything down and she reads the annual reports.

I would like to point out the obvious: she is a woman. Being a young woman interested in investing in the 1960s was difficult and Ginny explained it in the perfect way. "If you didn't go out and play cribbage with the other ladies then you got frowned upon. There were some things you had to do. You weren't yourself. You were a Mrs. Somebody."

Investing is a useful skill for everyone to have. It doesn't require leaving the house, therefore even "house wives" back then could use investing. You need money, a sense of risk and a sense of numbers, which are things the majority of people have, including 1960's "house wives."

Ginny taught me a lot about being a female investor. You have to stand up for yourself and work twice as hard to get the same treatment. My experience with her was very inspiring. I asked Ginny what was the biggest mistake she made with investing and what she learned from it. She responded with confidence, "Everybody makes mistakes and I haven't done anything horrible."

What Time Can Do for You

When Ginny married into her husband's family she acquired some of her husband's holdings. His grandfather would give everyone shares of the company he worked for, Otter Tail Power Company, for Christmas every year. Slowly, she became more and more interested in the fun and power of investing.

Ginny's main tip was to keep track of everything that you have bought, sold or looked into. Ginny said, "Before she would write things down to remember them but it is very important to not solely rely on someone else, like a stockbroker, to keep track of your stocks."

Her second tip was to invest in things she knows and believes in. In the time that I talked with her I heard many stories about many breakthrough stocks. Ginny says the best way to get a good feel for a stock is to read the company's annual reports, and keep up with their activity.

One of my favorite stories about Ginny is when she thought she was dying. Her relatives drove her to the hospital and while she was laying in what she thought was her deathbed she glanced over and saw the hospital tray: it was made by Kimberly Clark *(KMB)*. She said, "I did very well with that stock!"

I learned so much from her and she helps justify one of my investing beliefs. All you need is time and a good stock. She has a very humble, knowledgeable way of explaining investing. Time and again she said, "It doesn't take a math professor to know how to invest, and I am no mathematician." Now, as a 90-year-old she is learning Algebra because as a high schooler she was never given the chance to learn anything after Geometry. With age, she knows what investing path she wants to go down, and how to get herself there despite the roadblocks.

After mentioning all these companies, she has been successful with, we should look at their current numbers. Obviously, they all have grown and changed since she bought them, but this is what they look like now.

Companies	Price to Earnings Ratio 20 or lower	Dividend Between 2-5%	Gross Margin 25% or higher	Return on Equity (ROE) 15% or higher	Debt 1.0 or lower
Otter Tail Power Company (OTTR)	24.0	3.33%	43.2%	9.5%	0.7
Kimberly Clark (KMB)	22.0	2.79%	36.5%	—	—
Sherwin Williams (SHW)	26.0	1.08%	49.0%	87.3%	1.2
Pepsi (PEP)	24.8	2.74%	55.1%	54.7%	2.7

Numbers accurate as of February 2017
Source Morningstar

Ginny Has a Bone to Pick with Warren Buffett

I wanted to review the stocks Ginny mentioned during the interview. I didn't include all of them, but these are ones that stuck out to me. If we look at the current data we can see that they all, with the exception of Sherwin Williams, passed the same number of hurdles. All these companies have three things in common. They all have higher P/E ratios, some dividend, and very good margins. From this we can get a taste of what Ginny looks for in a company and her investing values. Some

112

of her values are buying stocks that are meant to be held for long amounts of time, buying high quality companies and finding high paying dividend companies.

Noticing her love for dividends brings me to another story. As most investors do, I idolize Warren Buffett. I asked her opinion of Berkshire Hathaway. Her quick response was surprising. She said, "If he isn't going to give us dividend, why would I buy his stock?" She previously owned Burlington Northern, a train company, and was not too happy when a dividend free investor bought the company. Before Berkshire Hathaway bought Burlington Northern, Burlington was a dividend paying company, making the adjustment even harder for her. Ginny lives off her dividends and has no interest holding something that won't pay her back in cash over the short term.

Now that we've looked at the current state of each company we will look at how much they've grown in 20 years. These companies were all held for different amounts of time, some longer than others and some shorter, but 20 years is a good estimate to show what time can do. I used Long Run Data[24] to find these numbers. Each company started out with an original investment of $1,000.

---

[24]www.longrundata.com/

Companies	Annual Return	Growth in 20 years with an original investment of $1,000 *(longrundata.com)*
Otter Tail Power Company *(OTTR)*	*9.09%*	$5,544.47
Kimberly Clark *(KMB)*	*8.18%*	$4,707.31
Sherwin Williams *(SHW)*	*14.48%*	$14,347.81
Pepsi *(PEP)*	*8.08%*	$4,617.18

Source Morningstar

Why Do You Invest?

I want to leave you with a very important story and question. As I said, when I walked in the door instead of interviewing her as I planned, she started interviewing me. After taking my coat off she asked me a very important question, *"Why do you invest?"* It took me awhile to come up with a thoughtful and honest answer. But Ginny says it the best, "Much better than slaving in a hamburger place."

This is a question that everyone should be asking themselves. *Why do you invest?* Whether you are just starting or have been investing for most of your life. ***Why do you invest?***

Accounts

"How many millionaires do you know who have become wealthy by investing in savings accounts? I rest my case." - Robert G. Allen

Types of Accounts

Money management is an incredibly important life skill. I believe putting your money into a bank can help with the ability to manage your spending. As a minor, you have a few options as to what type of account you want to keep your money in. I am going to talk about each one to explore your options. Keep in mind, this advice is meant to be used as another source of information. Everyone's financial situation is different. I am not a financial professional. Always do your own research!

Banking and Savings Accounts

As a minor, the first account I got was a savings account. As a minor, I would suggest $100 to start out, but any amount over that works as well. Savings accounts are simple: you put your money into a savings account at a bank and your money slowly gains a small amount interest. This is the easiest way, in my opinion, to start out with a bank account. Savings accounts are very safe, considering you leave your money in one place to grow, but it doesn't grow all that much. At the time of this writing, the average savings account has an annual interest of about 0.6%, which is not that much. If you put in $100 today, at that rate of interest, it would take about

116 years to double it (at $200). It depends on where you live and your bank because each bank (and state) has their own set of rules.

After I opened a savings account, I opened a checking account and was issued a Debit Card (age 14). Along with getting a Debit Card, you can also get an ATM card. The difference between the two, for those who don't know, is this: an ATM card is used solely to get cash from an ATM. You can only take out as much as you have in your account, same is true for a Debit Card. With a Debit Card, you use it like a Credit Card, but it will not let you go over your bank balance. For a checking account, you have two options: with interest or without. At the time of this writing, the annual interest for a checking account is around 0.5%. I would recommend having an account with interest, even if it is only a small amount. It takes a lot of time, but it slowly gives you more money.

Investing Accounts

Now that you've saved some money, let's look at some other accounts and even ones that let you buy stocks:
- UGMA (Uniform Gifts to Minors Act) or
- UTMA (Uniform Transfers to Minor Act) accounts,

They are both custodial accounts. This means that this account is under the minor's name and once they reach the age of 18 or 21 (depending on state laws) the account's completely under their control. If the guardian wanted to revert the account back to their name, for whatever reason, the guardian would have to pay taxes on the earnings.

The UGMA is used to transfer money to a minor that will be kept in their account. The UTMA on the other hand allows much more flexiblity. The minor can receive more than just transfers of money, they can get property, assets, *stocks* and other securities. Many parents don't tend to like custodial accounts because of the lack of control they have over their child's spending.

Educational Savings

A 529 plan is a qualified tuition plan meant for saving up for education. The money will grow tax-free while the money is kept in the account. And once it is time to take money out of the account for educational purposes you can take it out tax-free. That means that when you take out your savings from this account you don't have to pay taxes on it. With other accounts that are *not* tax-free, you would lose a large amount of money taking it out. As it applies to any other account, the rules vary depending on what state you live in. But with a 529 plan, you can enroll in any state, regardless of where you live in the country. They have an annual interest of 2%. This can monitor their spending as well as save money. As you get older there are more and more options open, but I believe it is best to start simple and go from there.

Roth IRA

A Roth IRA is a tax-free way to save for your retirement. The money put into your Roth IRA account has to be post income tax, but after that, as long as it is held in the account you don't have to pay taxes on it. You can add money to your Roth IRA as long as you have an income of any sort from a job.

One Click Away

You know why to save your money, open a bank account and how to find a stock, but one thing is missing: how to open a brokerage account? This is important because it is how you actually buy stocks. Here are three quick and easy steps to open a brokerage account and place an order to buy a stock. Consult a broker for more information.

Step One: Finding a Broker
A broker is a service. They stand between your stock and you. Depending on the company you are going with as your broker, the minimum opening balance and deposit fee is different. The minimum deposit can range anywhere from $0.00 to $2,500.00. One thing to look out for, is to make sure the minimum amount is an amount you can comfortably hold in your account.

Next, you need to know the fees the broker will charge you. You want to make sure that your broker's fee is low. For any investor, but especially a young investor it is important to have a low commission or fee when you buy and sell stocks. For example, if you want to invest $100, but the commission fee that your broker charges is $10, you just lost 10% of your money. Normally, the commission fee ranges from $5 to $10; the lower the better. For example, Fidelity and Schwab charge $4.95 and Ameritrade charges $6.95.

Step Two: Signing Up
Opening up an account will require a few things. Here are the most common items which may change depending on the service:

- Social Security Number or Tax ID Number
- Your Address
- Employment Status
- Drivers Licenses
- Annual Income or Net Worth
- Date of Birth

Step Three: One Click Away

Now that you have your account, you get to the best part of investing: buying a stock! Most broker's websites are set up the same way. First you have to find your company that you're investing in, which is what this book (hopefully) taught you. The website is pretty self-explanatory. Walking through it, it should have you fill out the ticker symbol of the company, whether you're buying or selling, quantity (number of shares) in which you are doing so, and your order type.

Depending on your order type, it changes the conditions of your purchase. This can be a little tricky. Your options are Market Orders, Limit Orders, Stop Orders, Stop-Limit Orders, and Trailing Stop Orders.

With most things in investing, the simplest is usually the best. The two simplest are Market Order and Limit Order. A Market Order means that your broker will buy or sell your share(s) at the best possible price during the business day. For most large, well-known companies with many millions of shares traded each day Market Orders will be the simplest for the investor. For more information visit Investopedia.[25]

---

[25] www.investopedia.com/terms/m/marketorder.asp

Next is Limit Order. Limit order is best selected when you are aiming for a certain price and the speed at which your shares are purchased or sold does not matter as much. The good part about a Limit Order is that you get to set the maximum price that you are willing to pay, and then you wait to see if your broker was able to fill your order. For more information visit Investopedia.[26]

Next there is the duration list. This tells the broker how long your order will be valid. You have two options here, GTC (Good 'til Canceled) and GTD (Good 'til Date). Good 'til Canceled means the order is open until you cancel it. Good 'til Date means that the order is open until a specified date in the future.

After you place your order, remember to check the order status to confirm that your trade went through at the price and amount you expected.

---

[26] www.investopedia.com/terms/l/limitorder.asp

Getting Started

Disclosure, I am not a financial professional. In ten years (or more) there are chances of each one of these companies will hard times at some point. I am in no way recommending the companies mentioned in any part of my book. These companies are examples to help you look and find ideas through another lens, that's it.

What's in your driveway?
Genuine Parts Co. (GPC)
O'Reilly Automotive Inc. (ORLY)
Polaris Industries Inc. (PII)
Tesla Motors Inc. (TSLA)
Tractor Supply Co. (TSCO)
General Motors (GM)
Ford (F)

What's in your kitchen?
American Water Works Co Inc. (AWK)
Coca-Cola Co. (KO)
General Mills Inc. (GIS)
Kellogg Co (K)
McCormick (MKC)
Mondelez International Inc. Class A (MDLZ)
Nestle SA ADR (NSRGY)
PepsiCo Inc. (PEP)
Rocky Mountain Chocolate Factory Inc. (RMCF)
The Hershey Co. (HSY)
The Kraft Heinz Co. (KHC)
Tootsie Roll Industries Inc. (TR)
Yum Brands Inc. (YUM)

What's in your pocket?
Alphabet Inc. C (GOOG)
Amazon.com Inc. (AMZN)
Apple Inc. (AAPL)
AT&T Inc. (T)

Discovery Communications Inc. C (DISCK)
Verizon Communications Inc. (VZ)

What's down the street?
Chipotle Mexican Grill Inc. Class A (CMG)
Costco Wholesale Corp. (COST)
Cracker Barrel Old Country Store Inc. (CBRL)
Dollar General Corp. (DG)
Dollar Tree Inc. (DLTR)
Dunkin' Brands Group Inc. (DNKN)
McDonald's Corp. (MCD)
Starbucks Corp. (SBUX)
Target Corp. (TGT)
Wal-Mart Stores Inc. (WMT)
Hennes & Mauritz AB ADR (HNNMY)

What's on your computer?
eBay Inc. (EBAY)
Facebook Inc. A (FB)
GameStop Corp. Class A (GME)
Lions Gate Entertainment Corp. (LGF.B)
Microsoft Corp. (MSFT)
Nintendo Co. Ltd ADR (NTDOY)
World Wrestling Entertainment Inc. Class A (WWE)
Walt Disney Co. (DIS)

What's in your medicine cabinet?
Johnson & Johnson (JNJ)
Procter & Gamble Co. (PG)
GlaxoSmithKline (GSK)

What do you play with (toys/sports)?
Deckers Outdoor Corp. (DECK)
Foot Locker Inc. (FL)
Hasbro Inc. (HAS)
Build-A-Bear Workshop Inc. (BBW)
Mattel Inc. (MAT)
Nike Inc. B (NKE)

Under Armour Inc. A (UAA)

Other:
Pricesmart Inc. (PSMT)
Clorox Co. (CLX)
Whirlpool Corp. (WHR)

Your Journey

Now that you have the knowledge to invest, I cannot wait for you to go out into the world and do it yourself! After you invest in your first stock, you are an investor, and that, no matter how old you are, is an accomplishment. I have some resources at the end of this book to refer to if you want to continue this journey.

Here are some things to remember:

You're going to make mistakes, everyone does. Don't let this discourage you. As an investor, you lose some, you win some, but your hope is that the winners outweigh the losers.

The younger you are the longer your hill! Start your snowball and let it roll! You're young! You have so much time, take advantage of your time.

With time, there is power. You are more powerful right now than you will be in a year. Invest in a world you want to live in.

There are so many successful investors in this world. They have blogs, websites, and other sources of information that is accessible.

I'm always here to answer questions or talk about stocks! If you want to talk hop on my blog (Compounding Snowballs) and comment, I'll get back to you as soon as I can.

My Journey

I was first inspired by Lauren Templeton and her story of herself as a young investor in her book The Templeton Touch. My first stop at the Berkshire Hathaway meeting in Omaha, NE, 2012 was the bookseller's area to have her sign my copy of her book and to meet my newfound idol. Sadly, for me, she couldn't make it to the event because she had just had a baby. Her husband, Scott Phillips, was very kind to me and handed me her business card after I verbalized my disappointment. As a ten-year-old, I didn't realize who I was talking to or where this would take me in the next five years. I wrote her a letter telling her how much I loved her sparkly business card and her story. That was how it all began.

Thank you to Lauren Templeton for being my mentor, and teaching me so much from her own personal story. She has been a true inspiration to me and I believe she will continue to be for many more women.

Thank you to LouAnn Lofton for inviting me to hear you speak about yourself as an early investor, for supporting my journey and projects, and always looking out for a fellow female investor. To this day, I remember sitting in the front row in a gray sweater, watching you speak about your newly published book, *Warren Buffett Invests like a Girl.* You inspired me to dive into investing, and I am incredibly thankful for everything it has brought me.

Thank you to David Gardner for my first one on one talk with a professional investor regarding Amazon's potential in 2013. We are now witnessing the growth and power many of the companies we talked about way back when.

Thank you to Tom Gardner for taking a chance on a ten-year-old for your College Women and Investing program and flying me out to D.C. to meet many motivating investors.

Thank you to Todd Wenning for always supporting and promoting me, along with everything you have done for *Early Bird*. Thank you for editing, sending feedback, and being interviewed. I definitely could not have done this without you.

Thank you to Hope Nelson-Pope for helping me with my first published blog post. I learned more than I could imagine from one very grueling editing experience, and I always try to channel you when I write.

Thank you to Bill Mann for teaching me and the readers about international investing, and giving me my first lecture about the power of investing way back in 2013.

Thank you to David Kretzmann for talking about early investing with me, and taking the time to share your inspirational story.

Thank you to Alyce Lomax for helping me since day one. I cannot believe that, four years ago, we were only chatting over email about me visiting the Motley Fool for my first time. Without you, I wouldn't have stepped foot in the Motley Fool or have been lucky enough to have the experiences I have had.

Thank you to Sam Davidson, David Kretzmann, Jason Mosher, Cheryl Palting, Amy Dykstra, and the others on the team for giving me a super fun project for the summer. I loved jumping into every meeting ready to learn and help on a range of things from giving kids the power to invest to the repercussion of spraying hand sanitizer in your eye.

Thank you to Beth Lily for always looking out for female investors and inviting me to attend one of your lectures at St. Thomas.

Thank you to the Motley Fool and all of your employees for helping people across the world invest foolishly and invest better.

Thank you to Buck Hartzell for giving me more reading for the plane ride home from D.C. and talking about the newest stocks with me.

Thank you to Saurabh Madaan for being a welcoming and thoughtful host when you invited me to speak to Google's investing club about kids and investing and my last book. I cannot wait to come back and talk about this book.

Thank you to Noah Schwartzberg for helping me think outside of the box about promotion, pushing me to make this the best that I can, and calling me back so I could learn more than I ever knew about the publishing process, branding, and the power of passion.

Thank you to Ginny Adams for spending a long afternoon with me, sharing your stories as a female investor, talking about Algebra II with me, and sharing your extensive amount of knowledge on investing.

Thank you to Mrs. Atchison and Mr. Schwalen for pushing me as a writer and helping me grow more than I ever knew that I could.

Thank you to Dave Hage, Debbie Hoak, and Seema Anwar for taking time out of their lives to edit this book. It really helped me grow as a writer!

Thank you to Kristin and Farhang Kassaei for hosting Just Dance at your house as a stress-relieving exercise after my talk and being two of my greatest supporters.

Thank you to Adrian Lane for attending all of the Berkshire Hathaway meetings with us, trying to convince my mom to get a dog, talking about stocks with me, sending warmth from Arizona, and as always, supporting me. You have been a crucial part of my journey.

Thank you to Boppy, Nana, Grammy, and Grandpa for always cheering me up or getting on me about buying the wrong thing. Thank you for supporting me in ways I never imagined I would need and always being interested in what's happening with my book now.

Thank you to my mother and father for being my biggest cheerleaders, sharing my love for investing and puns, and giving me the mindset of a fighter. I love you both dearly.

Thank you to Soren Peterson for being the best little brother I could ask for. You always inspire me to work my hardest and do my best. I am forever grateful to be your sister.

Finally, thank you to all my family and friends that have supported me through this process and have kept me on my toes, whether it was about a biotech penny stock you thought would be successful, enduring my endless lectures to buy Berkshire Hathaway, obsessing about a certain retail stock, or just laughing at our mistakes. You have all been an inspiration to me and there is no way I can thank you all enough.

Appendix - Case Studies

Case Study 1 - Mattel and Hasbro

Stocks	P/E Ratio	Yield	Net Margin	ROE	Debt	EPS
Mattel (July 2015)	12.7	3.73%	13.3%	27.8%	0.5	1.08
Mattel (June 2017)	27.7	6.86%	5.19%	11.8%	0.9	0.80

Source Morningstar

Looking at the data of then versus now you can see that there is a difference. Mattel had kept its dividend payout going over the past three years, but recently, Mattel's new CEO Margo Georgiadis said that they are lowering their dividend payout ratio from 160% to between 50-60%[27]. Mattel will end up paying shareholders a 15 cent per share dividend compared to their previous 38 cents per share dividend. Georgiadis will use this money to modernize products and Mattel's brand. She plans to build websites, video games and other online services to go along with almost all of Mattel's toys to keep up with the generation. I believe this will help with another

---

[27]www.wsj.com/articles/mattel-slashes-dividend-as-ceo-frees-funds-for-turnaround-effort-1497465249

target audience along with maintain their current customers which will be helpful for business. Mattel's new interest in expanding their technology side of the business is tracked back to their new CEO. Georgiadis recently joined Mattel's executives from Google.

Stocks	P/E Ratio	Yield	Net Margin	ROE	Debt	EPS
Hasbro (July 2015)	13.4	3.01%	7.9%	21.3%	0.6	3.57
Hasbro (June 2017)	24.3	1.92%	11.34%	33.0%	0.6	4.50

Source Morningstar

Hasbro has had success with the movie business. They continue to make deals with up and coming movies and are still maintaining contracts with Disney and Star Wars.

Stocks	P/E Ratio	Yield	Net Margin	ROE	Debt
Hasbro (June 2017)	24.3	1.92%	11.34%	33.0%	0.6
Mattel (June 2017)	27.7	6.86%	5.19%	11.8%	0.9

Source Morningstar

Case Study 2 - Moats

You should look for companies with larger moats but be prepared to pay a little extra for them. It is better to pay more for a good or great company with a moat than pay cheaply for a bad company. I will list all the companies with their metrics below.

Companies	P/E Ratio	Dividend	Gross Margin	Return on Equity	Debt
BNSF Railway (BRK.B)	18.7	---	---	8.2%	0.4
Chipotle (CMG)	142.0	---	15.2%	6.5%	---
McDonald's (MCD)	26.2	2.50%	42.3%	521.4%	---
Mastercard (MA)	31.5	0.68%	---	75.4%	0.9
Tiffany & Co (TIF)	25.9	1.93%	62.4%	15.0%	0.3
Barnes and Noble (BKS)	143.0	8.39%	31.3%	0.7%	---
Amazon (AMZN)	181.7	---	35.6%	14.2%	0.4
Coca-Cola (KO)	31.9	3.13%	60.9%	26.1%	1.4

Numbers accurate as of June 2017
Source Morningstar

Further Readings

Blogs:

Compounding Snowballs by Maya Peterson
(compoundingsnowballs.blogspot.com)

A Wealth of Common Sense by Ben Carlson
(awealthofcommonsense.com)

Clear Eyes Investing by Todd Wenning
(cleareyesinvesting.com)

The Motley Fool (fool.com)

Books:

Growing Money by Gail Karlitz

The Motley Fool Investment Guide for Teens: 8 Steps to Having More Money Than Your Parents Ever Dreamed of by David Gardner and Tom Gardner

Warren Buffett Invests like a Girl by LouAnn Lofton

Investing the Templeton Way: The Market-Beating Strategies of Value Investing's Legendary Bargain Hunter by Lauren Templeton and Scott Phillips

Keeping Your Dividend Edge by Todd Wenning